Fifty more years of the

HALIFAX

1953 – 2003

Richard Barrow

Published by Richard Barrow 2006
Fern House, Old Lane, Ripponden, West Yorkshire HX6 4PA

ISBN: 0-9552983-0-X
ISBN: 978-0-9552983-0-1

Typesetting, Design, Printing and Binding
The Amadeus Press
Ezra House, West 26 Business Park,
Cleckheaton BD19 4TQ

ACKNOWLEDGEMENTS

The author thanks HBOS for access to its archives which has provided valuable historical information and also for providing funding which has enabled this book to be published. The author would like to make it clear that the opinions and views are solely those of the author and are not views or opinions expressed by HBOS or members of the HBOS Group.

Many people have provided willing assistance in one form or another but special mention should be made to Hannah Watson for her gift of copies of Round the Table from 1945 onwards. Roy Pickard, Calum Macaskill and Sir James Birrell all provided much relevant background information, both verbally and in printed form. The Building Societies Association and the Council of Mortgage Lenders were also most helpful in the provision of historical factual information. Final thanks must go to my old colleague John Walsh and also Sian Yates of HBOS Group Archives who both spent considerable time in proof reading the book from both a grammatical and factual viewpoint.

CONTENTS

1

INTRODUCTION

In many ways Fred Dawson was typical of so many of the people recruited into the Halifax during the 1950s and 1960s. He was a bright lad from a working class background, educated at the local grammar school, which he left at the age of 16 with a string of good 'O' levels. He was naturally influenced by his dad, and had he been born a decade earlier he would no doubt have followed in his footsteps and gone to work in one of the local coal mines. However, this was 1964 and Fred Dawson had heard that the Wakefield branch of the Halifax Building Society was looking to take on two school leavers.

After sitting the Halifax's own examinations in English and Mathematics he was duly offered one of the available positions. Harry Howe was the branch manager and was regarded as belonging to the 'old school' – well known in the local business community and capable of running his own branch in a pragmatic manner. A simple example of Harry's practical approach to life was that, on occasions, he would bring his terrier dog into the office and tie it up to one of the legs of his desk. It was often thought that the way prospective mortgagees got on with his dog had a significant bearing on whether their application was successful. Harry observed that Fred suffered badly from acne and therefore put the other recruit to work on the counter whilst sending Fred upstairs to work on the agency ledgers, and therefore out of sight from the customers.

By 1967 Harry's retirement was imminent and Fred's acne was much improved thus allowing him to work on the counter. Harry's judgment was that Fred would not get on with the new manager and that it would be sensible for him to see if he could get one of the new jobs working with the recently installed computer at Head Office. As things turned out Fred did not get on with his new manager but he did get offered a job as a computer operator. In February 1968 he started work at the computer building in Trinity Road, Halifax, which is where I first came across him six months later when I too joined the Society.

In later years Fred became well known as a speaker on the local after dinner circuit, especially at rugby club functions. One of his opening jokes related to the fact that he came from Dewsbury and if his audience didn't think that was bad enough he had to work in Halifax! The message was that Halifax, like so many other northern towns, had passed its best, and was now full of empty shops, and run down factories and mills.

However, the post-war Halifax I grew up in as boy was a vibrant industrial town. When he was Chief Executive, Jim Birrell would often tell visitors that after the war the town of Halifax had five industrial or commercial enterprises that could truly be regarded as the biggest of their kind in the country. These were Asquith machine tools, Mackintosh toffees, Crossley carpets, Paten and Baldwin knitting wools and the Halifax Building Society. He would then go on to say that only the Halifax Building Society could still lay claim to this status. Today that claim is no longer true but Halifax plc is still an extremely large business and employer that undoubtedly brings great benefit to the town.

The significance of the Halifax Building Society to me as a young boy was immense. The Halifax Building Society office was the place outside which schoolboys returning home from Halifax to Skircoat Green caught the number 31 bus. Whilst waiting for the bus we would often mischievously mimic the

ROUND *the* TABLE

Staff journal of the
HALIFAX BUILDING SOCIETY
NUMBER 73   DECEMBER 1953

Front cover of *Round the Table* staff journal December 1953, depicting Permanent Buildings, the headquarters of the Halifax Building Society.

cries of 'Courier and Guardian' from the news vender who used to stick copies of the newspaper into the metal concertina gate drawn across the corner entrance of the closed building. When the office was open we gazed in through the windows, invariably speculating as to how much money was kept inside this great building. Our perception was simple and totally wrong. We knew little about the mortgage side of the business, our view being that it was just a sensible place to take your money for safe keeping, which once handed over was kept in safes down in the basement to be returned when the need arose. We comprehended the concept of interest but did not understand how it was funded. Above all we knew it was the biggest building society in the world because all the adverts said so, and that was something to be proud of for anyone who came from Halifax.

Railway bridge in Sowerby Bridge, which for many years had an advert on it depicting the Halifax Building Society as the 'Worlds Largest Building Society'.

(Courtesy Steve Gee)

Once a year I would read reports in the newspapers about important people from the Halifax Building Society going down to London to announce their annual results. These announcements always seemed to

7

feature quotes about how much bigger the organisation had grown after the completion of yet another record year. We did not understand it, but because we believed it had more money than any other similar organisation in the entire world, we held it in the highest esteem.

The years went by and in September 1968 after going to university and spending a year with VSO in South America I came back home to Halifax and was in need of a job. The Halifax looked a good bet so I applied and was successful in obtaining a position of trainee programmer in their computer department. Timing and an element of luck are what are needed in life and I was fortunate to find myself working in information technology and also for a financial services organisation, both of which were set for spectacular growth in the coming years. By the mid 1970s I was in charge of a small technical team, which amongst other things had responsibility for the development and support of the software for the branch terminal systems. During this time a significant development was the use of ATMs or cash dispensers, as they were then known. The Halifax was at the forefront of their introduction within the UK building society movement with the installation of several IBM 3614 lobby machines during 1978.

There were many companies trying to enter this market in the early days, some coming from a background of supplying safes, eg Chubb in the UK and Diebold in the USA, and others coming from supplying computer equipment to the banks eg IBM and NCR. The public's initial slow acceptance of these machines coupled with their poor reliability meant that it was not until 1983 that the Halifax installed a full function 'through the wall' ATM. This was obtained from Diebold but was purchased through Philips, our main supplier of branch terminal equipment. Although these machines gave good service they were not without problems, especially the way the notes were presented to the customer via the use of a drawer. Ever mindful of keeping abreast of what was happening in the marketplace we had had a dialogue with NCR since 1985 and had followed with interest their success in selling to the major banks. Indeed we evaluated one of their machines in 1986, which worked well, but decided to stay with Philips/Diebold for reasons of economy of scale.

The ATM market was experiencing rapid change when on 2 October 1990 John Gilroy of NCR came to visit, his aim being to bring me up to date with their latest products which he hoped eventually to sell to the Society. I looked forward to seeing him as we were genuinely interested in their ATMs, especially as our existing supplier (Philips Business Systems) had recently lost the right to market the American Diebold ATMs. We were having trouble with Philips in getting the support we needed to cope with the dispensing of the used and very poor quality banknotes we were being supplied with by the clearing banks. Following the usual discussions on the banking and building society industry at large John suggested that it might be a good idea to revisit the NCR plant in Dundee to view their latest developments. This plant was the largest of its kind in the world, and it had acquired this pre-eminent status due entirely to the single-minded leadership of an amiable Scot called Jim Adamson.

Jim Adamson had been headhunted back in 1980 when the production line had been halted because customers (notably Barclays) were refusing shipments owing to quality problems. On the face of it he had inherited a disaster plant with a cynical workforce and a management that did not accept responsibility. He, however, saw great potential in the product and immediately started to work long hours, communicating with his management team on his belief in quality. Within six months he had resolved the immediate technical problems and averted disaster as the production line started to roll again. He then started to focus on the next generation machine that he believed would need to be more reliable by virtue of better design and quality control in manufacture. He spent hours talking to as many customers as possible about what they saw as their main priorities in an ATM. If Jim Adamson was in his office and a customer was visiting the plant (and there were often several on any one day) there was every chance that they would meet him and be quizzed regarding their requirements.

After glancing through the diary, which was filled with the usual series of meetings, the idea of a visit to Dundee seemed eminently sensible. I decided to take with me three other colleagues who had experience of our ATM network and who would also enjoy a drink and laugh in the bar at night. Hence Fred Dawson, Dave Platt, Peter Butters and myself set off from Halifax at three thirty in the afternoon on 20 November to cover the 280 miles to Dundee. Why on earth did we leave it so late to set off? Someone had kindly slotted a six-hour budget review meeting into the earlier part of the day meaning we would definitely be ready for that drink once we got to Scotland! We sped off up north on what proved to be an uneventful journey and met up with John Gilroy at the hotel at half past eight. A table was booked for nine o'clock at the Old Mansion House hotel in nearby Auchterhouse, which left little time for a wash and making the odd phone call.

At quarter to eleven it was too late to move off to a local hostelry. We instead retired to the hotel's library where we sank into some deep-seated sofas and were served with coffee, with orders being taken for that long awaited pint of 80 shilling, or in Fred's case another pint of Guinness. The group was tired but in good heart and Dave Platt got up to take a closer look at the bookshelves. After a minute or so he uttered a cry and pulled out a pale blue bound book, which had a title indicating that it was about

Left to right: Fred Dawson, Dave Platt, Richard Barrow and Peter Butters
still enjoying a drink together 15 years after their discovery of
'Hobson's A Hundred Years of the Halifax'

Halifax. This was of immediate interest to Fred, Peter and myself as we were all Yorkshiremen and Dave, being a Lancastrian, promptly handed the book over. Fred opened the book and was amazed to find that it was not just a book about Halifax but was a book about the Halifax Building Society. Fate had indeed had a hand in the day's proceedings and we spent the next hour marvelling at the contents of Oscar R Hobson's *A Hundred Years of the Halifax*.

We, like many other Halifax employees, were all company men and were surprised but proud that a book could have been written about our Society in 1953 and that a copy of this book should survive for nearly 40 years and turn up on a book-shelf in farthest Scotland. The appendices at the back were of particular interest - appendix XI for example being a list of the chief executives and staff as of 1 February 1952. Even though the book had been written many years before we had started at the Halifax the number of people we knew or recognised astounded us. I am afraid that night we were somewhat unsociable to our NCR hosts as we continued to pore through the book – there was some speculation as to whether it had been a clever marketing ploy by the NCR sales team to plant the book in such a strategic place. We did think of 'borrowing' the book but being good honest 'Halifax' employees we replaced it on the bookshelf. It was going up to one o'clock by the time we rolled into bed back at our hotel.

Nine o'clock next morning saw us all on site and after a brief introduction and update we embarked on a tour of the plant. One particular area was testing out a new carbon fibre cash cassette, the old metal model having being identified as a source of reliability problems. A lot of these problems were attributed to the harsh treatment the cassettes received at the hands of the security firms, who transported them to and from the bank branches. The people involved in the testing were pleased to relate that Jim Adamson had been to see them, asking various questions about how robust the new cassette would be. At the end of this questioning he got hold of one of the cassettes and threw it up into the air as high as possible, letting it smash down onto the concrete floor. The cassette survived undamaged but the exercise was yet another example of Jim Adamson's practical approach. We returned to the briefing room prior to lunch and our eventual departure back to Halifax.

It was no surprise to find Jim Adamson there waiting to see how we had got on and what new developments we had in mind for the Halifax. What was a surprise, however, was that he presented me with Oscar R Hobson's book duly inscribed 'To Richard on your visit to NCR Dundee. Best of luck. Jim Adamson NOV 90'. He had obviously checked up first thing in the morning to see how the visit was going, been told about the book discovery and immediately despatched someone to buy (or probably be given!) the book from the hotel. As far as I am concerned the book has become a prized possession as well as a reminder of Jim Adamson's marketing skills.

Jim Adamson's inscription inside Hobson's book

Although by nature I am a slow reader, by the end of the following weekend I had read the book from cover to cover. I was even more impressed now than I was on first discovering the book. One could not help but have a sense of pride in the organisation, with particular admiration for its early leaders, Jonas Dearnley Taylor and Sir Enoch Hill, who between them steered the Halifax through its first 85 years. Other, slightly older, colleagues who had been with the Society in 1953 were a little surprised that I had no previous knowledge of the book. They, along with everyone else who were in the Society's employment back in 1953, had all been given a copy. The book documents the great changes that occurred during the Society's first 100 years and my thoughts have often centred round how important it is that the more dramatic changes and growth that has taken place during its next 50 years should also be documented. Destiny, experience and circumstances have dictated that I am in a position to perform this daunting task. Whilst the views expressed must by nature be somewhat personal, I also hope that it provides an accurate account of the next 50 years in the Halifax's development.

Following on from our visit, Jim Adamson came to see us in Halifax on 27 February 1991. We had half an hour's chat with Mike Whitehouse in his office, the conclusion of which was that we would finally buy some NCR ATMs. The first lobby ATM was installed in Worcester in November of the same year, followed by the first through the wall ATM at Elland in the February of the following year. These ATMs from NCR were the first of several thousand that the Society was to install. Jim Adamson's visit concluded with the usual tour of our technology developments including a visit to the Conserv-a-trieve automated deed store. He indicated that he had a mortgage with the Halifax and enquired whether it would it be possible to examine his title deeds. Although he had no idea of his roll number we were quickly able to perform the appropriate terminal enquiries and deed request. After a minute of further discussion we walked over to the relevant workstation by which time his deeds had been extracted and were waiting for him. Although this technology belongs to the less glamorous back office administration area, Jim Adamson was undoubtedly impressed by the efficiency of the Halifax organisation. I feel sure that he would be pleased to know that he has had an important influence on the writing of this new book.

2

100 YEARS OLD

1953 was an eventful year – Hobson's book had been published, the Halifax was 100 years old and the nation celebrated the coronation of Queen Elizabeth II. The Halifax was justifiably proud of the progress it had made since its formation and celebrated by giving all staff a £20 bonus, awarding all subscription shareholders an additional 0.25 per cent centenary bonus and finally by organising several parties, including one held in the Alexandra Hall, Halifax on 4 February. This date was the actual anniversary of the Society's formation and invitations for the Alexandra Hall party were sent out to the 'staff and their wives of Head Office and 53 northern branches. It is interesting to note the

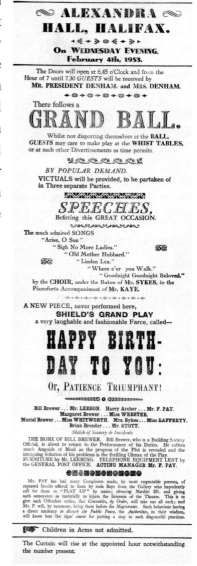

In HONOUR of the CENTENARY of the HALIFAX BUILDING SOCIETY.

❧ ALEXANDRA ❧ HALL, HALIFAX.

On WEDNESDAY EVENING, February 4th, 1953.

The Doors will open at 6.45 o'Clock and from the Hour of 7 until 7.30 *GUESTS* will be received by **MR. PRESIDENT DENHAM. and MRS. DENHAM.**

There follows a

GRAND BALL.

Whilst not disporting themselves at the **BALL**, *GUESTS* may care to make play at the **WHIST TABLES**, or at such other Divertissements as time permits.

BY POPULAR DEMAND.
VICTUALS will be provided, to be partaken of in Three separate Parties.

SPEECHES,
Befitting this GREAT OCCASION.

The much admired SONGS
"Arise, O Sun"
"Sigh No More Ladies."
"Old Mother Hubbard.'
"Linden Lea.'
"Where e'er you Walk."
"Goodnight Goodnight **Beloved.**"
by the **CHOIR**, under the Baton of **Mr. SYKES**, to the Pianoforte Accompaniment of **Mr. KAYE**.

A NEW PIECE, never performed here,
SHIELD'S GRAND PLAY
a very laughable and fashionable Farce, called—

HAPPY BIRTH-DAY TO YOU:

Or, Patience Triumphant!

Bill Brewer ... Mr. LEESON. Harry Archer ... Mr. F. PAY.
Margaret Brewer ... Miss WEBSTER.
Muriel Brewer ... Miss WHITWORTH. Mrs. Sykes ... Miss RAFFERTY.
Brian Brendar ... Mr. STOTT.
Sketch of Scenery & Incidents

THE HOME OF BILL BREWER. Bill Brewer, who is a Building Society Official, is about to return to the Performance of his Duties. He suffers much Anguish of Mind as the progress of the Plot is revealed and the intriguing solution of his problems is the thrilling Climax of the Play. FURNITURE by Mr. LEEMING. TELEPHONE EQUIPMENT LENT by the GENERAL POST OFFICE. ACTING MANAGER Mr. F. PAY.

Mr. PAY has had many Complaints made, by most respectable persons, of repeated Insults offered to them by rude Boys from the Gallery who impudently call for them to "PLAY UP" by name; throwing Marbles &c. and giving such annoyance as materially to injure the Interests of the Theatre. This is to give such Offenders notice, that Constables, by Order, will take out all such; and Mr. P. will, by summons, bring them before the Magistrates. Such behaviour having a direct tendency to disturb the Public Peace, the Authorities, in their wisdom, will know best the legal course for putting a stop to such disgraceful practices.

☞ Children in Arms not admitted.

The Curtain will rise at the appointed hour notwithstanding the number present.

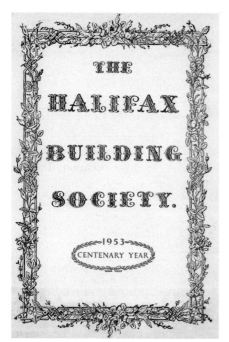

THE HALIFAX BUILDING SOCIETY.

~1953~
CENTENARY YEAR

Official invitation to the centenary party

100 Years Old – The Centenary party as depicted in Round the Table

term 'staff and their wives' rather than 'staff and partners' and reflected the role of women in the Society at the time. All female staff were either single women or widows, there being no part for married women to play in the running of the Society.

The May 1953 edition of *Round the Table*, the staff journal of the Halifax Building Society, reported in detail on the event:

> Everybody received a programme typographically resembling the style in vogue a century prior. This announced a grand ball and provision for the non-dancers to disport themselves at whist tables or indulge in such other divertissements as time permitted. It assured them that victuals would be provided and that the speeches would befit the great occasion. The Society's choir would render several admired songs under the baton of Mr Sykes with Mr Kaye providing pianoforte accompaniment. A very laughable and fashionable farce 'Happy Birthday to You' from the facile pen of Mr Arnold Shield was to be performed.

In his speech, Algernon Denham, the President, traced the history and growth of the Society during its first 100 years. For his part, Fred Bentley, the General Manager, said that in his opinion the most important decision which led to the development of the Society was the one to decentralize the accounting system and allow district managers increased responsibility.

Of all the many words spoken regarding the Society's progress during its first 100 years, this observation of Fred Bentley's was one of the more astute. Many years later John Spalding, who was Chief Executive during the 1980s, related a similar observation. He quoted a conversation he had with the Chief Executive of the Derbyshire Building Society who laughingly observed that whenever the Halifax opened a branch in new territory it 'went in and colonized the area'.

The Halifax branch managers undoubtedly had much more authority than their counterparts in other building societies. Not only were they responsible for their own accounting they were also responsible for the distribution of their mortgage quota as well as managing the agencies in their area. The Halifax manager was a man of some standing in the town who would have good contacts with the solicitors, accountants, insurance brokers, estate agents and valuers in the area and would use the good name and marketing clout of 'the biggest building society in the world' to bring in the business.

In contrast the competitors' branches were often more akin to the Halifax's agencies where their counter sheets of transactions would have to be sent off to their head offices for posting to the relevant accounts. Customers were willing to queue in a Halifax branch to conduct their business whilst they could have used a competitor's branch across the road that was empty and was possibly offering slightly better interest rates. The best analogy is that of a busy restaurant where diners wait for a table rather than risk a meal at the empty restaurant next door.

Lending long and borrowing short was the basis of the building society movement and many a business analyst would claim this mismatch to be a risky proposition. There were however inbuilt mechanisms that greatly reduced this risk, one of the main ones being the use of liquidity. The liquidity of the Society was used as a buffer, which could be enlarged if there was good investment inflow but poor demand for mortgages, or it could be reduced if the investment inflow was poor but the demand for mortgages was good. However, increases or decreases in liquidity could only go so far before further investment money was refused or mortgages were rationed or stopped altogether. The Society had seen both these situations during its first 100 years resulting in a temporary slow down in the growth of assets, this being no great problem for a mutual organisation.

The products on offer to the Society's customers in many ways reflected the early concepts and share values (one share still being £120) on which it was founded. Deposit accounts attracted an interest rate of 2 per cent and depositors would have first call on the Society's assets should the Society have to be wound up. Paid-up share class 2 had full member status and attracted an additional 0.25 per cent interest. Subscription shares were a regular savings account where the customer was committed to save up to 10 shillings a lunar month (or 10s 10d a calendar month) for a full share or as little as 2 shillings a lunar month for a fifth of a share. Depending on the prevailing interest rates the subscription share would mature after around 14 years when it could then be transferred into a class 1 matured subscription share account. These subscription share accounts had the same rate of interest as class 2 accounts but were also paid an annual bonus as decided by the board, eg 0.5 per cent in 1954. Members were encouraged to open several passbook accounts and come into the branch to use the counter on a regular basis where they would undoubtedly have a chat with the cashiers – slightly different from the emphasis of today where the phone, Internet and electronic transactions are strongly encouraged. Of particular importance was the status of the class 1 matured subscription share account that had a red colour passbook and indicated to others that its owner was worth at least £120. Very similar to having a gold or platinum credit card today!

The lending side of the Society's business was very much influenced by the after effects of the Second World War, by politics and by the cautious, conservative culture of the Society. On the existing pre-war housing stock the Society would only lend up to 175 per cent of the pre-war valuation even though the vacant possession valuation would often be 300 per cent of that valuation – much less should the property have a sitting tenant. This limit was put into place because the Society believed that property values would settle down to around 200 per cent of pre-war values and also that borrowers should always find a reasonable deposit for their property out of their savings.

After the war, the bulk of new residential building was undertaken by local authorities, thus supplying more houses for the rental market. Private house builders were tightly controlled on how many houses they could build, who they could sell them to and for how much. Until the new Rent Act of 1957 rents were severely restricted leading to a situation where tenants were paying well below a true economic rent if the property was kept in good order. This situation encouraged many tenants to remain in cheap rented accommodation and discouraged the role of the private landlord. There was thus a restricted call on the Society's funds that led to substantial loans being made to small businesses such as restaurants and cinema chains along with the maintenance of a high level of liquidity.

However, by 1953, with the Conservatives in power, things were changing as was reported at the Society's 1954 annual meeting where mention was made of the Society being 'pleased to see the lifting of restrictions on building houses for owner-occupiers'. The figures quoted for new houses built for such purpose were 22,889 in 1951, 35,712 in 1952 and 70,045 in 1953. By the autumn of 1954 mortgage lending was beginning to be restricted, payment of introductory commission for mortgages was suspended and loans were limited to a maximum of three times salary. This was the start of a mortgage quota system for branches that was to last, on and off, for the best part of 30 years.

The employees of the Society, many of whom had been in the forces during the war or had been away on national service, were experiencing the increasing freedom of post-war Britain. This broadening of outlook was often at conflict with a somewhat strict office regime. New recruits at Head Office found an environment that was very similar to the school they had just left. Serious bad behaviour such as nipping out of the office to visit the local shop could result in 'expulsion' from the office for three days. Such lads (lasses would never do such things) could often be seen wandering round Halifax town centre killing time and taking a drink in the café in the borough market, for they had left home at the normal time in the morning not daring to tell their parents of their fall from grace.

Getting married was also regarded as a serious business and for female staff it was very serious, as it signalled the end of their career with the Halifax. Male members of staff had to obtain the permission of the

General Manager or his assistant and if you were under the age of 25 you were regarded as not being old enough or wealthy enough to take on these new responsibilities.

Geoff Fearnley, who had been at Head Office since leaving school in 1945, recalls being interviewed in 1954 by Assistant General Manager, Edwin Beresford. The interview was regarding his request to get married at the tender age of 24 to a Margaret Sutcliffe. Fortunately for Geoff it emerged early on in the conversation that Margaret's father was a pig farmer from Holmfield. This was of immense interest to Beresford who also lived on a working farm at Mytholmroyd where all the animals he kept were noted for being black and white. The remaining conversation centred solely on pigs and Geoff was duly given the all clear for the proposed marriage.

However, consent was by no means automatic as another young lad of 20 found when his girlfriend became pregnant and he decided to do the honourable thing and marry her. The Society regarded him as being too young to get married and he therefore had to leave. This was maybe a lucky break for the lad as he ended up having a very successful career in the police force. Mike Whitehouse at the age of 21 was a young computer programmer at Head Office in 1968, but even then he still had to write to Eric Leeson in staff department telling him of his impending marriage to Helen Bowers. Leeson told Whitehouse that he thought he was too young, Whitehouse told Leeson that that was a matter of opinion and Leeson replied that no it was more a matter of experience. They still got married; Whitehouse deciding to ignore the advice of senior management.

The division of roles and responsibilities between the board and the executives in many ways had changed little in 100 years. The most startling fact by today's standards was that there were no executive directors, not even Fred Bentley the General Manager had a place on the board. The board met every fortnight and its composition was the great and the good of Halifax with the odd director coming from as far away as Leeds, Manchester or Sheffield. The total fees payable for all directors was £1,056 for the quarter end 31 October 1953, somewhat modest by today's standards even after allowing for inflation.

The Halifax board of directors 1953

The composition of the board at its anniversary was as follows:

A Denham (President)
D H C Briggs (Vice President)
H Cowan Douglas
L Crowther
J Hunter
Sir A L Mowat
R W Tolson
W Turner
Lord Riverdale
Sir E N Whitley.

The last two directors had been asked specifically to stay on the board to see the Society through its centenary but were to resign in April 1953 because of 'advancing years' ie, they were both in their eighties. They had been on the board for 34 and 17 years respectively and were replaced in May by Ian A D MacLean (Crossley's Carpets) and John H Denham (son of Algy Denham). The following summary of the board minutes for 2 September 1953 gives an indication to the level of detail that was reported to the board:

◆ Bank account - balance £5,000,000.

◆ Liquid funds - £40,000,000, which roughly equalled 20 per cent of assets. These liquid funds included £1,000,000 National War Bonds and Corporation Loan Stocks of £25,000,000.

◆ Statement of operations - receipt and payment totals for the period to date. Investors department balance £190,000,000 and borrowers department £160,000,000.

20

◆ Salaries – total bill for August 1953 - £41,624 8s 8d.

◆ Loans to local authorities - eg Manchester Corporation £150,000 over seven years at 4.25 per cent.

◆ Application for exchange of shares - this was a mechanism for giving a re-advance to carry the debt back to the amount of the original advance and was used for loans to businesses such as shops, joiners, cafés and cinemas.

◆ Enquiries for advance - a list of all mortgage enquiries over £4,000.

◆ Consent to lease - a list of all requests to sublet parts of properties in mortgage to the Society, eg subletting upper part of shop for £60 a year.

◆ Borrowers repayments - 928 mortgages of initial advance value of £484,373 had been repaid in the period.

◆ Suspension of subscriptions - agreement had been given to suspend subscriptions on 34 accounts of total balances of £24,384.

◆ Communications - agency appointment and branch acquisitions. Also included was the following analysis of applications for advance for the year ending 31 July 1953:

61% - counter   6.5% - insurance companies
19% - solicitor   1% - builders
12% - estate agents

◆ Staff matters - included district manager appointments and increases in salary as well as appointment and termination of solicitors to the Society's panel. An analysis of mortgage accounts which had been repaid which quoted amongst other data 8.97 years as being the average life of a mortgage. Also mentioned were the venues for the forthcoming branch conferences namely:

Portsmouth   Bristol
London (Waldorf Hotel) Manchester
Halifax (Alexandra Café) Glasgow
Birmingham

◆ Miscellany - a copy of a letter sent to the Abbey congratulating it on reaching £200 million assets.

As can be seen, everything of any operational significance was reported to the board. In December 1953, £3,605 was quoted as being the cost of producing Oscar Hobson's centenary book. At their meeting on 4 January 1956 the board learnt that a new billiard table for the sports and social club had cost £150 and on 5 June 1957 they were informed that the Head Office heating bill was £3,893 for the year. Every year the cost of producing the Society's diaries was reported, eg for 1957 14,000 diaries at 3s 10½d each plus 30 per cent purchase tax costing a total of £3,526 5s. There was always, of course, a series of letters from individual staff members thanking the board for salary increases and staff holidays.

The vast amount of operational detail dealt with by the board and the decisions required meant that it had to meet fortnightly which was still the case up until 1978 when the meetings were then changed to the third Wednesday of every month. Even then, however, a board member was still expected to sit on one of the various subcommittees that met on the first Wednesday of the month. As well as the operational running of the Society, the board was also heavily involved in competitive and strategic matters.

The directors at their meeting on 1 August 1956 discussed the transfer of the engagements of the Braintree and Bocking Building Society (assets of £296,000) whose directors 'felt that they, along with many other small local societies, had outlived their purpose'. Indeed it seemed that the takeover of a small society was a regular annual event during the 1950s, these societies being happy to transfer their members' interests to the Halifax where they knew they would be well looked after. Changes in the income tax composite rate were discussed in detail as they obviously had an effect on the Society's interest rate structure. During the 1950s composite rate tax (tax paid on investor's interest) was around 25 per cent (4s 10d in the pound in 1955, 5s 4d in the pound in the 1956) this being of great benefit to higher rate taxpayers.

More impressive, however, than all this mass of detail in which the board was involved was the way they saw themselves as being at the head of a social movement, bringing benefits for the ordinary man. The language that they used gives us a good indication of the way they regarded themselves – 'we as *custodians* of your organisation', '35 years *service* to the Halifax', 'a leading influence of the *movement*'. This constant reference to the building society movement gave the impression of belonging to something that was very much akin to a religion.

The board saw it as their responsibility to spread the word and educate the great British public about the benefits of belonging to a building society. Even though mission statements were unheard of in those days the Halifax had an implied one which was often quoted and was quite simply **'to further the cause of thrift and home ownership'**. Back in the 1950s many customers and indeed staff did not fully appreciate the concept of a mutual organisation and the significance of its growing financial reserves (these being the accumulated yearly surpluses, or profits, of the Society). However, Denham certainly did and he brought a somewhat conservative approach to the management of the Society's finances feeling that it should also give a lead to the rest of the movement. One yardstick that he used was the Society's liquidity, and here he was difficult to please as can be seen from his comment at the 1956 AGM:

> You are well aware of your Board's policy on liquidity and our ratio of 15.31% is reasonably adequate.

One got the feeling that Denham would have preferred to have done less mortgage business and kept the liquidity at the post-war ratios of over 20 per cent. However, an even more sensitive issue was the reserve ratio (ratio of reserves to deposits), which if it were to be maintained would either limit the growth in assets or require an increased profit margin from the existing business. Denham's statement to the 1954 AGM summarised his attitude:

> In recent years it has been customary for us to report a record accretion in our assets, but I would repeat that nothing is further from our minds than to seek size. Your board prefer gradual and controlled progress with unimpaired strength to unduly rapid growth at the expense of the reserve ratio.

At their meeting on 21 March 1956 the directors had before them a comparison of the reserve ratios of the top 15 building societies, the first six of which are reported below:

| Building Society | Reserve Ratio | | Average Share | Average Deposit |
	Market	Book	holder Balance	Balance
Halifax	4.49%	4.49%	£558	£253
Abbey National	3.94%	3.48%	£390	£1196
Cooperative	3.15%	2.51%	£434	£1208
Woolwich	4.2%	2.51%	£542	£293
Leeds Permanent	5.27%	5.19%	£838	£243
Alliance	2.09%	1.04%	£826	£1392

These figures not only show the Halifax in a good light regarding its reserve ratio but also highlight the fact that the Halifax was the only society to report the book value of its reserves. The average low deposit balance also indicates the Halifax's reluctance to accept large deposits, which it regarded as being 'hot money' that could easily be withdrawn, should interest rates become uncompetitive. Halifax's large number of small investors was seen as a great competitive strength and again this was reported at the 1956 AGM:

Our policy of cultivating the small investor continues unaltered. Our average inestment is £470 compared with £448 last year and the total of investments upon which we are liable for income tax at the standard rate[1] is only £2,733,153.

Denham knew exactly the strength of the Halifax – it was not only the biggest but it was unique in that it had got to that position the hard way by developing a network of substantial branches which supported a vast number of small, loyal investors. In spite of his comments about not being interested in size and growth, the marketing slogan of the organisation remained 'the biggest building society in the world'. The concern in the 1950s was to give the borrowers, who may be limited in numbers, the best deal possible. As we shall see later he was not afraid to use the financial muscle of the Halifax to encourage the rest of the movement to do likewise.

[1]*Standard rate income tax was paid on all individual investments that were greater than £5,000.*

3

THE 1950s

The split in roles, responsibilities and power between a board of directors and its executive is invariably unique but must work well for the continued success of an organisation. We have seen that the board of the Halifax in 1953 was extremely powerful, albeit that because of the age and infirmity of some members it must be accepted that the real power rested with President Algy Denham. The fact that the board had tremendous power does not mean to say that they always used it. Because of the vast amount of data reported to them, decisions on such matters as 'enquiries for advance' for example must in general have gone through 'on the nod'.

The real power for such matters often lay with the executive and branch management. However, the fact that an item such as the appointment of a new solicitor to the Society's panel had to go to the board will have undoubtedly made the person making the recommendation think twice. Even on major issues such as changing liquidity ratios the General Manager could often lead the board. This, however, was not the case with all matters, the level of staff remuneration being a good example!

Over the years the Society had created a mechanism for reporting all this data to the board. The procedures and systems in place to do this and also control the branch network reflected the fact that administration was yet another of the Society's great strengths. Even though all the transactions were posted to ledgers held at the branches the entire mortgage offer administration was performed centrally at Head Office.

Agenda type room was responsible for producing the board agenda that included many sheets containing enquiries for advances. As a follow on to these enquiries the type room was also responsible for producing all the mortgage offer documentation. Elizabeth Carling, who was in charge, recalls the department employing up to 60 girls, some on a part time basis. The board agenda was produced on huge foolscap sheets on typewriters with an especially long carriage. Tippex, never mind a word processor, was unheard of which meant that the typing had to be accurate first time. Checking and rechecking ensured there were no mistakes, the papers having to be with Fred Bentley by half past four on the day prior to the board meeting. Elizabeth recalls the exasperation of using the duplicating machine to get all the copies of the board papers. If the machine was not broken it seemed to end up dispensing purple ink onto the girls and herself – purple ink smudges on a girl's hands and face being a very good indication that she worked in agenda type room.

During periods of little mortgage lending Elizabeth had to go round the other head office managers seeking work and if none was found the girls could then get their knitting out. Other departments such as endowments, building mortgages and of course deed administration reflected a central Head Office control of the Society's main asset – its mortgage book. The 250,000 deeds that the Society had custody of in 1953 were regarded as of immense value, being kept in secure rooms in the basement of the Head Office building. In those days it was a legal requirement of the Building Societies Act that the auditors examined each deed, as this was regarded as essential documentation for the security of the mortgage loan.

Whilst mortgage applications and repayments were largely administered centrally, the investors' business was mainly branch controlled. In 1953 all Head Office functions and a counter for customers were located in the Permanent Buildings, Commercial Street, Halifax. In this building the investors' department looked after all the administration and ledgers associated with these local customers. On top of this the department was also responsible for providing technical advice to all the other branches and updating the branches' investors general instructions. In 1953 the administration was all manual and a large proportion of that work was geared around the processing of investors' transactions. The vast majority of transactions took place at the counter where they would be written into the passbook and onto a counter sheet. There were different counter sheets for all the different investors' departments (deposit, paid-up shares class 2, paid-up shares class 1 and subscription shares). These counter sheets were then passed to the back office where they would be used to update the individual customer's ledger sheet.

The calculation of investors' interest was particularly time consuming and was done on an annual basis, half yearly interest being brought in during the early 1960s. Interest was calculated on a minimum monthly balance, receipts gaining no interest until the following month, unless they were received in the first three days of a month. Withdrawals would affect the minimum monthly balance unless they took place during the last three days of the month. The calculation of the annual interest and writing it into a customer's passbooks was by any standard a huge logistical exercise. Remembering that the Society's financial year-end was then 31 January, customers could bring in their passbooks for the crediting of this interest any time after 3 January. They were given a receipt for their book and this would be available for collection on or after 14 February. Given the fact that there was no financial advantage in collecting a book on this date it was difficult to comprehend the length of the queues in the branches on the first day they were available for collection. It must have been a matter of 'seeing is believing' and it also gave the more numerate of the Society's customers something to check.

Staff were only paid 95 per cent of their salary as a normal monthly payment, the remaining 5 per cent being paid as a bonus during the first three months of the year. This bonus was intended as remuneration for the extra overtime and effort required to perform this investor's interest exercise, a payment system that was still in place when I joined the Society in 1968. Obviously it was something of an anomaly in the payment of most Head Office's specialist departments but I remember well that the first 60 hours of overtime worked in a new year was not paid, it being deemed that you had already been paid for this with the 5 per cent bonus. Certain younger staff from Head Office were also sent out to local branches to assist with the interest calculation, although it was debatable how committed they were given the fact that they did not have to live with any mistake they may have made. It was a time of the year that certain staff hated but customers looked forward to, especially if they were also to receive an extra 0.25 per cent bonus for holding a share account. The most respected members of the Society were also often given a calendar and diary at Christmas.

Head Office had the expected central departments of finance, personnel, legal, marketing etc, along with branch support functions such as premises and agencies. Branch inspection department had an important role in ensuring standards did not slip in what was a large devolved organisation. The inspection team would turn up unannounced, often at the start or end of the working day, their first job usually being to count the cash making sure there were no IOUs in the till. They were there to check on the branch's administration as well as any potential fraud. The posting of transactions and interest to passbooks and ledgers, property insurance renewals and the branch index of customers by name were amongst the major items that were checked.

Staff who had previously held an assistant branch manager appointment formed the backbone of the inspection teams and this experience was seen as being excellent training for their next career move, which would be to run their own branch.

Two other men who had been brought into the Society on a 'fast path' in 1951 were also listed as being inspectors in 1953. They were Raymond Potter (JRLP[1]) and Albert Thayre (AJT), both of whom were graduates. Potter had previously been the secretary of the Royal Institute of International Affairs and Thayre had worked as head of the investment research department of a leading firm of stockbrokers. They had been brought in from outside to counter any claims that the top management of the Society was too incestuous and it was generally accepted by all parties that Potter was the more senior of the two recruits. They had both reached the level of lieutenant colonel in their army career and somewhat confirmed the belief that successful promotion in the forces during the war led to subsequent success within the post-war Society.

The list of executives in 1953 did show that others had been brought in from outside such as Alexander O Thomson, the Chief Accountant, and Donald W Bromley, the Head Office solicitor. They did however stand alongside life-long servants of the Society such as Edwin Beresford (started 1914, and a nephew of Enoch Hill who was General Manager 1903-1938) and Cyril H Greenwood, Chief Inspector (started 1926). The list of branch managers for 1953 reflected the fact that before you became

---

[1] Both Potter and Thayre were commonly referred to by their full initials JRLP and AJT.

a manager of even a modest branch of four staff you would have been in the Society's employment for at least 20 years. If you achieved the position of branch manager by the time you were 40 you were doing well and no doubt you would have had to work at several different branches along the way. It was unwise to refuse promotion to a different branch, as there was no guarantee that a similar offer would be made in the future.

Not everyone took to this somewhat authoritarian regime but it did offer job security along with numerous other benefits. Payment was modest with a scale in operation starting at £140 at the age of 16, going up to £600 at the age of 32. From then on employees were 'off scale' with pay being reviewed annually or on promotion to a new management position within the branch network or Head Office. Loyalty and long service were thus encouraged and one was deemed to have a career with the Society rather than having a job that had a fixed payment rate. Increments in salary could be obtained for studying and passing exams for shorthand and typing along with the Charted Institute of Secretaries and the Building Societies Institute.

Subsidised mortgages were regarded as a significant benefit with a staff rate of 4 per cent which some years later went up to 5 per cent or half the public rate, whichever was the lower. There was, however, an upper limit to the amount of the advance that attracted this advantageous staff rate, this again being on a scale that was dependent on salary. The fact that the mortgage funds would be available for staff without the need to go on any waiting list was also a great advantage when negotiating a house purchase. On investments there was again a staff rate that equated to the top rate being paid on subscription shares.

One of the benefits that could be applied for, demand often exceeding supply, was to go on a staff holiday. These holidays were heavily subsidised with the Society paying up to two thirds of the cost and were always of a high standard including some quite exotic locations. For example in 1953 not only were there family holidays to the Devon and Yorkshire coasts but trips to Belgium's Heyst and Italy's Lake Como. The Society's staff magazine, *Round the Table*, reported that the trip to Lake Como was seen off from Victoria Station by Mr Jennings the London

Strand branch manager. After 24 hours of train, boat and coach journeys across four countries, the Halifax party arrived at their destination. The many excursions that took place included visits to Milan and Venice. Observations were made regarding the picturesque poverty of the ramshackle collection of peasant houses around the lakeside (bear in mind this was only eight years after the Second World War). This indeed was some holiday even by today's standards and it was reported, as was always the case, that there was an 'expression of thanks to the Society's Directors for their generous assistance in making this holiday possible'.

A senior member of the party was allocated as leader who would ensure that no really bad behaviour took place, liaise with the tour representative and would also have to write the subsequent article for *Round the Table*. Joyce Barlow remembers a trip to Oberammergau when she was in her late twenties. One evening four of them arrived back at the hotel just after midnight and needed to ring for the night porter in order to gain entry. Next morning they received a severe reprimand from the party leader and were forbidden to go out on their own again.

Obviously even these bargain holidays came at a price, especially if you regarded a holiday as a total break away from the work environment. Others, however, enjoyed the fellowship of work colleagues and families and often managed to get themselves onto another holiday in subsequent years. Amazingly these holidays kept going until 1976, albeit in the later years they catered mainly for those wanting a UK family holiday.

Head Office also had a properly constituted sports and social club with an annual meeting chaired by the General Manager. The social events included coach outings to far away places such as York and Knaresborough, dances and whist drives at the Alexandra Hall and a Christmas party for the children of members of staff. All of the functions organised by the Society were of a high standard and staff, partners and children attending such functions were always in their best 'bib and tucker'. Whatever children thought of the Christmas party they needed no persuasion to attend. The reason for this was noted in 1954 by Mrs Raymond Potter who reported in *Round the Table* that:

Father Christmas met with the usual measure of approval, and the handsome presents which he distributed caused one to wonder what rate of interest the Wenceslas Building Society was charging.

In October of each year the 'staff function' was held at the Alexandra Hall and invitations were given to all members of Head Office and to branch staff on a rota basis as there was not enough room for everyone and, of course, cover was required to man the branch network. Branch staff travelled the length and breadth of the country to attend and those from distant branches were put up in local hotels overnight. Supper was provided and as usual people could partake in dancing and/ or a game of whist. Speeches were given and the President's Cup was presented to what was judged to be the best kept branch. The Head Office choir would often entertain and in 1953 there was a new addition of a staff handicrafts exhibition. There were no alcoholic drinks provided and it was therefore common to see a brisk trade in the town's pubs during the evening as many of the male attendees 'nipped out' for a quick one. This was a situation that was rectified some years later when Potter decided it was time to have a licensed bar and this was affectionately referred to as 'Potter's Bar'. The following day parties of branch personnel were shown round the Head Office departments prior to returning home.

On the sporting front in 1953 *Round the Table* includes references to table tennis, snooker, swimming and football and golf competitions organised by the West Yorkshire Building Societies' Sports Association. There was also an annual bowls competition held at Spring Hall in Halifax

Staff holiday of 1956 to Norway

31

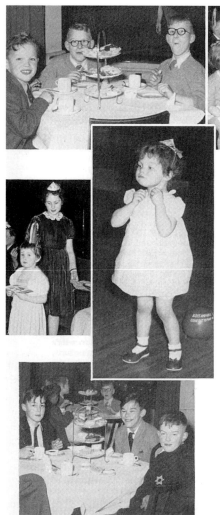

CHRISTMAS PARTY

Mrs RAYMOND POTTER

I THINK that the photographs on this page show most effectively how much the Sports and Social Club Children's Party on December 22nd was enjoyed. The food, the entertainment (official and otherwise) and the pleasant surprises all clearly met with the full approval of both grown-ups and children. Indeed the absence of any worried frown on the expression of the principal organiser, Mr R. E. Weston, was in itself an indication that all was going well.

The thanks of all of us are due to Mr Weston, Mr Kaye, and others and in particular to the young ladies of the staff who so charmingly and competently relieved the mothers temporarily of their parental duties.

This was the first occasion on which I and my four children were privileged to attend this annual party and we were most impressed by everything — not least by the magnificent arrangements for the appearance of the day's most welcome visitor, Father Christmas, met with the usual full measure of approval, and the handsome presents which he distributed caused one to wonder what rate of interest the Wenceslas Building Society was charging.

And so to the sound of bursting balloons and cheerful laughter, another most enjoyable party came to an end.

1954 Children's Christmas Party

playing for the Howell trophy. However, it was the cricket section that seemed to be the most active and get the most coverage. They played in the West Riding Building Societies' League as well as several friendly matches such as married men versus single men, Head Office versus Manchester offices and men versus ladies. Indeed the ladies' cricket section appeared to take the game seriously, dressed in white skirts and blouses along with proper cricket pads.

Ladies' cricket was obviously a tradition within the Society as the March 1956 edition of *Round the Table* includes an old picture of a 1926 ladies' cricket team posing with Enoch Hill at Greetland, Halifax. In spite of all these activities, the sports and social club never had quite the same standing as clubs that were attached to other large local employers (eg Crossley's Carpets) or other building societies (eg Leeds Permanent). These invariably had their own stand-alone facilities, along with a licensed bar and steward.

Ladies' cricket teams of 1926 and 1955

In the early 1950s the Society turned down the opportunity to purchase Spring Hall mansion and playing fields from Paten and Baldwin who were using this site for their own sports and social club. In 1956 the directors did provide funds to obtain a lease and convert some rooms in Horton Street, Halifax into a club for playing snooker, table tennis, darts, cards and watching TV. The venture was half hearted and again did not have a licensed bar and steward and was regarded by those who used it as a 'bit of a dive'.

Part of the sporting history of the Society, but run separately from the

Three players, including Harry Howe on the right, at the 1957 Golf Circle finals at Fixby

sports and social club, was the Golf Circle competition. This started in 1930 when Sir Enoch Hill was Circle President. In those days the final was held at Halifax Golf Club at Ogden, which Sir Enoch captained for a few years. By 1953 the Golf Circle had a membership of 612, there being 31 qualifying rounds for staff and associated business contacts. There were 35 solicitors, six surveyors, five agents and 12 members of staff taking part in the final at Huddersfield Golf Club at Fixby, the prizes being presented by Algy Denham, the President. Expenses and overnight hotel accommodation were paid for by the Society and the whole event was viewed as excellent corporate entertainment for the Society's business partners.

Young lads working at Head Office sometimes had the chance to have half a day's paid leave in order to caddy for the finalists. Refreshments for these caddies were thrown in but any payment was at the discretion of the golfer. The Golf Circle continued to be an important event up until the 1990s, always getting centre page coverage in *Round the Table*. Not all of the chief executives in the last 50 years had the same love of the game as Sir Enoch Hill, but there were enough golfing senior executives such as Calum Macaskill and Nigel Watson to ensure its continuing popularity in its later years.

In describing how the Society functioned at the end of its centenary the focus so far has been on the Head Office environment, but as has already been mentioned the branch network was the jewel in the crown of the organisation. Again *Round the Table* gives us a good insight into branch life. Much mention was made of branch buildings being converted or renovated to 'bring them up to the Halifax standard'. Bradford Bank Street branch reported: 'The reinforced glass windows inserted after war damage are to be replaced by plate glass, the better to display advertising material'. Branches such as Plymouth reported on the reconstruction of their city centres and their branches in the eight years since the ending of the war.

Branch display windows became a major marketing initiative in the post-war years, prizes being awarded for the best displays. Branch location was all important, many sites being reassessed following major post-war city centre developments. Similarly, the Society had high standards when it came to agency premises, always preferring good, ground floor locations.

As has already been mentioned, agencies were controlled directly by the Society's branches, which received through the post the agencies' completed counter sheets. Visits were required by branch staff to agencies to replenish stationery stocks and also perform audits. Holding agency conferences and organising agency visits to Halifax for the AGM encouraged identity with the Society. An interesting report from the Southend branch in 1953 mentions the disastrous floods in which they lost two members of staff and also of the loyalty and dedication of their Canvey Island agent:

> Mr H Redman, the Society's agent on the island, spent several unpleasant hours on his garage roof watching the flood water carry away his coal bunker. His cash till was soaked. He dried and ironed the pound and ten shilling notes before handing them over at the district office.

Sports and social functions at the branches were similar to Head Office, large branches such as Glasgow inviting nearby branches to attend their dances. Visitors from other branches and Head Office were genuinely welcome and the spirit of belonging to the Society is portrayed by this 1954 Bradford Sunbridge Road report:

> It is with great regret that we learned of the accident which our Mrs Graham had whilst on her motoring holiday in Scotland, and we are very grateful to our friends of the Edinburgh staff for their kindness to her during her enforced stay in the Royal Infirmary there.

Mrs Graham has written most appreciatively of the kindness of the members of the Edinburgh staff, who have visited her regularly during their free time, and have greatly cheered her with their friendly conversation and thoughtful gifts. She makes grateful mention also of the flowers and other gifts received from her friends at this and the Bank Street offices.

She also says how very pleased she was to receive visits from the Assistant General Manager, Mr E Beresford, and from Miss P Haigh of the Bradford (Bank Street) office.

It is a great tribute to an organisation so large and widespread as ours that a member of staff can write, as did Mrs Graham – 'I feel very happy and proud to be on the staff of the Halifax'.

There were always plenty of farewells and welcomes of new staff to report, particularly young girls who were leaving to get married, to be replaced by a new batch of even younger girls. One can see how so many marriage partners were found in the workplace of the Society. Lists of staff who had obtained a new appointment, retired, reached 25 years' service or passed a relevant examination all helped to keep the branch people informed and give them a sense of belonging to the Halifax.

After 100 years, the Society had grown into a most impressive organisation. The management style was paternalistic and everyone who worked for it had a feeling of belonging to a large family. Unfortunately, like many families, there could be fallouts. The Halifax was about to experience just such a fallout, and in a very public way.

4

THE FRED BENTLEY AFFAIR

Even though nearly 50 years has elapsed there are many people in Halifax (and beyond) who can recall the 'Fred Bentley affair'. To understand fully the background to the affair one needs to go back to Sir Enoch Hill's time. In 1928 the merger took place between the Halifax Permanent, the largest building society, and the Halifax Equitable, the second largest. By the time the Second World War had started, the assets of the merged society had nearly tripled and 100 new branches and agencies had been opened. The 'Halifax', as the merged organisation was called, was a colossus in the building society industry and remained so until it converted to a plc in 1997. Its growth had been achieved the hard way by encouraging the smaller investor and borrower, this being deemed to be fundamental to building society principles.

Many small societies were content to accept the situation of the Halifax being a dominant force. Their interest rate strategy was often to track the Halifax but offer an extra 0.25 per cent or 0.5 per cent premium on investments and should their organisations have to be wound up they were often happy enough to be taken over by the Halifax. The problems arose with the middle ground societies who were more independently minded but who in truth had no chance of operating in the same league as the Halifax. Sir Enoch Hill was aware of the sensitive issue of branch expansion and argued that experience showed that a new Halifax branch not only made good itself but also stimulated the appetite for building society services in general. The Halifax publicity machine in selling the benefits of thrift and home ownership also brought business to rival societies.

One of the advantages that building societies had over the banks was the composite rate of income tax paid on all personal investments below £5,000. The operation of the scheme involved a sampled investigation of societies' investors, providing the Inland Revenue with details of account balances and interest paid. This information was supplied by all societies to the Inland Revenue who then used this data to work out what tax would have been paid by the individual investors. Some investors would have been subject to the full rate of income tax whilst others would not pay any tax at all.

For all these individuals an average or composite rate of tax was calculated which would then be levied on all societies' investors. It is open to some conjecture how accurate or thorough this large complicated logistical operation was and there was undoubtedly some final bartering between the Inland Revenue and building society officials as to the rate which would be applicable for the coming year. This rate varied but was always below the standard rate of tax – eg for 1955 to 1956 the composite rate was 4s 10d in the pound whilst the standard rate of income tax was 8s 6d in the pound. Thus the less well off, sometimes referred to as 'widows and orphans', who were not paying any income tax were in effect subsidising the better off who were paying tax at the standard or higher rates. These 'widows and orphans' would have been better advised to invest in National Savings where their interest would not be taxed at source, but such was the marketing appeal of building societies, especially the Halifax, that they still attracted their funds.

The Halifax had a policy of not accepting more than £5,000 in total from any individual and this was enforced by the use of a 'pink card' signature card index that listed all the accounts at a branch for a given customer. It was the branches' responsibility to ensure that any credit to any of a customer's accounts did not take their total investment with the Society above the £5,000 limit. Adherence to this policy and system was sacrosanct as if it was found that more than £5,000 had inadvertently been accepted from a customer the Society was liable to pay income tax on any interest at the standard rate – this being an extra cost to the Society rather than the customer. Other societies, however, were much more relaxed about attracting large capital sums (hot money) especially from companies; the interest paid on such investments being taxed at the standard rate. This was seen as an easy way of growing the assets of a society but had the disadvantage that these funds were very interest-rate sensitive and could be easily withdrawn.

A further problem for societies that grew rapidly by attracting hot money was the reserves of that society would have to support a larger asset base, with a subsequent reduction in its reserve ratio. In contrast the policy of the Halifax was for steady organic growth supported by a healthy reserve ratio. As previously mentioned, the reserve ratio for the Halifax in 1956 was 4.5 per cent and compared well with the Cooperative and Woolwich at 2.5 per cent and especially well with the Alliance at 1 per cent. It was the Halifax's policies on hot money and reserve ratios, and its desire for the movement to follow its lead, that led to its major disagreement with the Building Societies Association (BSA) during the 1950s. The BSA was the industry's trade body and the only specific obligation on its members was to adhere to its liquidity regulations (minimum of 7.5 per cent in 1956), any contentious issues being dealt with by persuasion and education.

After the 104th AGM in 1957, Algy Denham asked Donald Bromley, the Head Office solicitor, to put on record the sequence of events that had taken place leading up to Fred Bentley standing for election to the Halifax board. This document was titled 'The Hundred and Fourth Year', was 116 pages long and was filed for safe keeping with the board minutes. In this document Bromley states that after the Enoch Hill era:

While it may be an overstatement that the relationships of the Halifax and the Building Societies Association savoured of a 'cold war', they were certainly for the most part lacking in cordiality.

Denham and Bentley both believed in the role of the small investor and making home ownership available on the easiest possible terms. Denham was, however, more conservative in his approach to liquidity and reserve ratios and the use of hot

Fred Bentley General Manager
1949 – 1956

39

money. Bentley for his part was more a man of the people, seen as firm but fair and easy to get on with. He was not without ambition and it is understandable that he would want to pursue his work with the BSA, influencing its direction from within rather than by external confrontation. Bromley gives us a good insight into the workings of the BSA with his comments:

> The position of the members of the Council of the Association is curious and indeed must frequently occasion embarrassment to the members. It is aptly described in the words of the editorial to the Building Societies Gazette for July 1956 … 'A man is elected to the Council by the votes of members of the Association as an individual, and not as the nominated representative of his Society. Similarly, it is he personally, and not his Society, who is elected by his Council colleagues to the chair …. As spokesman of the Association he may publicly advocate one policy, but have to practise at the direction of his board a completely different line in his own Society.'

Whilst the last comment may have been true, if the differences in policy were great it would certainly not be easy to satisfy both roles. Differences there were, as is illustrated by the fact that in the 10 years from 1945 to 1955 the Halifax's investors' rate was lower than the BSA's recommended rates in nine of those years. Halifax's mortgage rate was usually the same as the BSA rate giving it a wider margin which assisted with the extra costs of supporting its relatively larger number of small investors.

At the start of 1954 Bentley applied to the directors for their consent to

his taking up the position of Deputy Chairman of the Council of the BSA. To be offered this position, which was seen as automatically leading to being Chairman two years later, meant that he must have been well respected by his colleagues at the BSA. Denham may well have had reservations about the Halifax supporting Bentley's candidature but nevertheless they did support him, showing the esteem in which he was held. It is unknown as to whether they thought that Bentley could change the BSA's strategy from within or

Algernon Denham President
1945 – 1961

40

that they could change it from the outside. What is not in doubt is that they had made a fundamental error of judgment and set a time bomb ticking, which, as events were to show, would be very difficult to defuse.

In the August of 1954 the board announced a reduction in the mortgage rate to 4 per cent as from 1 October, whilst others in the movement were charging 4.5 per cent. In pursuing this policy they were yet again showing that their number one objective was to provide 'home-ownership on the

Press coverage of the Halifax cut in mortgage rates to 4%

easiest possible terms'. This cut in rates was greeted as good news by the home buying public and received exceptionally favourable front-page coverage in the national press. The rest of the movement did not, however, appreciate the reduction, which they knew they could not emulate because the corresponding reduction in their investors rates would have a dire effect on their investment inflow. This lower Halifax mortgage rate meant unwelcome and fierce competition for any new mortgage business. Bentley, at least in public, supported the Halifax stance and in his editorial in the December 1954 *Round the Table*, mentions again the fundamental advantage the Halifax had by saying:

> Yet the Halifax, with an investment rate of 1/4 % lower than most other societies, continues to enjoy an inflow of funds adequate to enable progress to be made along the controlled and measured lines which the Board have long deemed prudent.

On 27 January 1955 bank rate moved from 3 per cent to 3.5 per cent making the Halifax 4 per cent mortgage rate look even cheaper. The demand for Halifax 4 per cent mortgages was such that embarrassment was being caused and various methods had to be devised to decline sound business in order to keep within quotas. In an interview with Denham on the following Saturday Bentley demanded that at the next board meeting the mortgage rate be raised to 4.5 per cent stating that the 4 per cent rate was 'disintegrating the movement'. Denham replied that while Mr Bentley would of course be free to give his views to the board he himself would resist a change for the time being.

At its meeting on 2 February 1955 the board decided to defer a decision on a move in interest rates, which resulted in an outburst from Bentley directed against Denham and by inference the rest of the board. This outburst came as a complete surprise and shock to the board, but they overlooked Bentley's behaviour on this occasion.

The situation resolved itself temporarily when bank rate rose to 4.5 per cent on 24 February 1955 and the Halifax moved to a 4.5 per cent mortgage rate and a 2.5 per cent investment rate which was in line with the movement. Bentley had demonstrated the difficulty in trying to 'wear two hats' and Denham had emphasised his and the board's power when it came to the setting of interest rates. Indeed it looked as if Denham was flexing his muscles and deliberately looking for a fight with the BSA rather than trying to smooth things over in the run up to Bentley's chairmanship.

The summer of 1955 saw a tightening on credit and dearer money resulting in building societies in general suffering a heavy fall in the net flow of funds with many societies ceasing to do any new mortgage business. The Halifax suffered much less than most due to the fact that its investment rates were now in line with the movements and also because of its policy of not accepting hot money. In spite of these poor trading conditions the BSA had hoped to stave off any increase in rates but in July they finally had to capitulate and at an emergency meeting recommended an investment rate of 3 per cent. The Halifax, along with some of the other leading societies, reverted to the nearly 'normal' situation of being 0.25 per cent less competitive at 2.75 per cent.

Denham did not let up in his campaign against the policies of the BSA. A letter was sent to them on 29 August 1955 concerning the use of hot money to satisfy the expansionist policies of certain societies. As a way forward it was suggested that an independent enquiry be set up (chaired by someone like Lord Balfour of Burleigh – ex Lloyds chairman, city editor of *The Times* and a partner in Lazards) to conduct an investigation into the affairs of the movement.

The BSA rejected Denham's suggestion preferring to sort matters out themselves. In November of 1955 a meeting took place between Denham, his Vice President, Donald Henry Currer Briggs, and Francis Lumb, the Chairman of the BSA. Little was achieved other than the invitation for them both to meet a special committee of the BSA Council at the Council's headquarters in Park Street London.

Time was marching on and the Halifax board were informed on 18 January 1956 that the selection committee of the BSA had stated that it was their unanimous wish that Mr Bentley should accept the nomination of Chairman. The board stalled for time in giving permission for this appointment stating that they were waiting for the outcome of the meeting at Park Street that had now been set for 8 February 1956 and which, they hoped would lead to a settlement of their differences. The meeting duly took place and Denham and Currer Briggs left with the definite impression that the BSA were aware of the importance of the points raised and were anxious to cooperate, especially with regard to recommending a ceiling of £5,000 on investments. This progress was reported back to the Halifax board on 15 February 1956 and at the same board meeting Bentley was given permission to take on the job as BSA Chairman.

The board heard nothing further until the receipt of a letter from the Secretary of the BSA dated 25 April 1956 in which was stated:

> Since I wrote to you on the 13th February 1956 the Council has given a great deal of thought to your suggestion for a maximum investment on the lines indicated in item 4 of that letter. After a great deal of thought the Council has, however, come to the conclusion that it could not see its way to make any recommendations to members on this point and instructed me to inform you accordingly.

Denham wrote a personal letter in reply dated 30 April stating that it would be some time before he could consult with his colleagues but he personally was very disappointed to find that no real progress had been made. He also included a paragraph (which Bentley later referred to as 'the offending paragraph') indicating that he felt that the meeting at Park Street had been a last ditch effort to solve their differences of opinion and to find a common platform which would enable the Halifax to remain in membership of the BSA.

This letter was put before the Halifax board at their meeting on 2 May where its contents were fully supported. The board expressed a wish that Denham's letter should be made available to the Halifax representatives (which included Bentley) and the Secretary of the BSA all of whom were at the annual meeting of the BSA in Bournemouth. Bentley took strong exception to the letter, which he had obviously not seen before. He informed the directors present at Bournemouth that unless the President withdrew 'the offending paragraph' before six o'clock the following evening (when he was due for election to the Chair) he would take the earliest steps to go into retirement from the service of the Society. Denham saw no reason to withdraw anything and Bentley, who was now the Chairman of the BSA council, duly resigned from the Halifax on his return from Bournemouth. Bentley reasonably expected that when the board endorsed his application for Chairman they would continue to be members of the BSA during his term of office. No doubt Denham would have argued that circumstances had changed but he certainly showed no evidence of 'live and let live' towards the BSA in order to support Bentley in his run up to taking on the BSA chairmanship.

Not surprisingly at their meeting on 6 June 1956 the board decided to give the requisite notice to terminate the Halifax's membership of the BSA, a period of exclusion which lasted until the December of 1964. Bentley proceeded to tidy up the details of his retirement from 40 years' service at the Halifax, refusing offers from the board of an office and secretarial help in Halifax to assist him with his BSA commitments.

At a presentation from the staff on 29 June to mark Bentley's retirement many kind and heartfelt words were spoken. In reply to these Bentley said he thought that the Halifax Building Society was a very great

Edwin Beresford presents a gift to Fred Bentley on his retirement

institution and he believed it would so continue and then concluded by quoting the words inscribed on the United Nations' building in New York, 'what is past is prologue' - prophetic words indeed.

Towards the end of the year the rumour became persistent that Bentley would stand as a candidate for election to the Halifax board at the next annual meeting. The board unsuccessfully approached the Deputy Chairman of the BSA Council to see if there was any way possible to dissuade Bentley from pursuing his candidature. His nomination was duly handed in on 18 February 1957 and was sponsored by the great and the good including F E Warbreck Howell, a former General Manager, and Eric Treacy, Archdeacon of Halifax. With stern Yorkshire determination on both sides this fight would have to be fought to a conclusion.

A position had been created on the board by the departure of John Hunter with three other directors, Donald Henry Currer Briggs, Hugh Cowan Douglas and Roger Tolson, retiring and standing again for re-election. With Bentley's nomination there were thus four candidates for four positions. However, in order to ensure that there should be a decision on Bentley's suitability for the board the directors reduced their numbers from 12 to 11, thus ensuring one candidate would be unsuccessful.

The directors thought that it was now time to disclose to members of staff the full facts surrounding the disagreement, information that up to that date they had refrained from disclosing. Meetings were held in several centres throughout the country, directors presenting the board's case to district managers and senior staff. Subsequently a six-page branch memo was also sent out reiterating the facts presented at these meetings, with managers being encouraged to inform agents and surveyors of the gist of this memo.

The national press had picked up on the story with many editors clearly favouring Bentley. Bearing in mind that there were no postal or proxy votes, steps were taken to accommodate a much larger attendance at the annual meeting. The venue was changed to the Victoria Hall, Halifax, which had over double the capacity of the Alexandra Hall where the meeting was usually held. Arrangements were made to accommodate any overflow in the Alexandra Hall, where they could hear the speeches over specially installed loudspeakers. Subsequently they could walk up to the Victoria Hall and vote.

A special train was laid on to bring members of staff, agents and surveyors from London to Halifax, an initiative that received certain adverse criticism. It had long been the practice to bring these people to the annual meeting and to pay their expenses, so with the increased numbers wishing to attend a special train was in fact cheaper than allowing individual travelling and hotel expenses. The other problem for the board was that they might well have normally hoped for the support of these people, but with a secret ballot this was by no means guaranteed.

The day of the meeting, 1 April 1957, dawned fine but with a cold wind blowing through the streets of Halifax. Yet long before the meeting was due to start members stood in their hundreds in the street outside the Victoria Hall waiting for the doors to open. When they did open it was quickly filled to capacity and it was necessary to use the overflow accommodation of the Alexandra Hall. Denham, the President, was in the chair and the normal business of receiving and adopting the director's report and balance sheet went through in record time.

The mayor of Keighley proposed the election of the three retiring directors. Pointing out the success of the Halifax's independent policy he stated that these three directors were entitled to the members' confidence and support. Mr J Lindsay Steel proposed the election of Mr Bentley which was seconded by Mr Ralph N Ross both men stressing the suitability of their candidate and quoting his 40 years' experience with the Society. Hilda Smith, F E Warbreck Howell and Archdeacon Eric Treacy all spoke in support of Bentley. Bentley then presented himself to the meeting explaining that it had not been his desire that any members of the then present board should be displaced.

If any one of the retiring directors were not re-elected the responsibility would rest with the board. He spoke of the difficulties he had experienced arising from the conflict between the Society and the BSA. He concluded by saying that if elected he would be able to work in harmony with his colleagues, and made no secret of his hope that the Society would soon return to membership of the BSA. The President then addressed the meeting, at some length, detailing the relationship the Society had with the BSA and the efforts it had gone to in order to resolve its differences. He summarised these differences as:

> Principal criticisms in recent years have been concerned with the granting of 100 per cent mortgages to 'sitting tenants', the intake of large capital sums from limited companies and the need for strengthening liquidity and reserve ratios.

The ballot then took place and when all the votes had been counted the results were announced:

F Bentley	1255 votes
D H C Briggs	1330 votes
H Cowan Douglas	1298 votes
R Tolson	1247 votes.

It could hardly have been closer with Roger Tolson losing out to Bentley by a mere eight votes. In all probability the reason for this was that with the names being put down in alphabetical order on the ballot paper Tolson's name was last and he therefore did not benefit from the few instances where voters had just gone for the first three names on the paper. Bentley concluded an eventful day by stating that:

> I hope this may be the end of a chapter, and not the beginning of a new one, with harmony prevailing.

Certain people present thought that Denham had gone on too long in his address and had consequently lost an element of the support that he may have had at the start of the meeting. Ironically at their June board meeting the directors increased their numbers back to 12 and Tolson was invited back onto the board.

What was the conclusion to these momentous events? Denham proved that he had the ultimate power when it came to setting interest rates and policy, but he lost the crucial vote at the annual meeting. Bentley lost his executive position but became a director, a position in which he was later seen to have little influence. Both men seemed to be living in the shadow of Sir Enoch Hill, but neither could match him in terms of charisma and leadership. Both were influenced by the importance of the BSA, yet neither could see that its importance was starting to wane. At the time there was a feeling amongst many of the younger managers that the Society should have grown the business by adopting an aggressive pricing structure, which would have been at the cost of reducing the Society's high reserve ratio.

Section from front page of the Halifax Daily Courier for Monday 1st April 1957
(*Courtesy of Halifax Courier*).

This sacred cow of maintaining a high reserve ratio was questioned some years later by the Hardie Committee in 1967. They found it difficult to justify some of the higher reserve ratios of the larger societies and proposed a sliding scale with the smaller societies having to maintain relatively higher ratios. So in a way Denham was correct in encouraging smaller societies to increase their reserves, but not in wanting the Halifax to have unnecessarily high reserves. His style of management was also far from open as is illustrated by his direct and secretive communication with the BSA, usually bypassing Bentley. He never got over the confrontation and his personal health suffered greatly resulting in him having to stand down in 1961, followed by his death in November of the same year. A portrait of Denham was commissioned in 1963 to commemorate his 39 years of service to the Society – the portrait still hangs on the walls of the committee room on the fourth floor of the Halifax Head Office.

Denham's image was that of a conservative financier with a high regard for the principles of the building society movement. Being Chairman of the Halifax was, however, not his only occupation, his other main interest being Bradford Property Trust (BPT) in which he was a substantial shareholder and Executive Chairman. BPT invested in residential property, traditionally buying whole streets of terrace houses and selling them to individuals, usually the sitting tenant - in effect buying wholesale and selling retail. They were at the forefront of using this business approach to the property market and went on to specialise in buying large residential estates from industrial concerns that had built them to house their workforce. In post-war Britain these firms found that there was a conflict of interest between the role of employer and landlord, with a rent increase often leading to industrial action in the factory. They were therefore more than happy to dispose of such capital assets that were giving a return of less than 2 per cent a year.

The business model for BPT can best be understood by looking at an initial venture of Fred Gresswell, one of the co-founders of the firm, who at this stage was operating on his own. His first 'wholesale purchase' was for 16 large back-to-back houses in St Stephens Road in Bradford for £95 each. One vacant house was immediately sold for £200 with the rest being offered to the sitting tenants for £135 each, a price that covered legal and surveying costs. Gresswell arranged a building society mortgage of £120 but also had to provide a second mortgage to cover the deposit as none of the tenants had any savings. The total expenditure for these former tenants was more or less the same as they had been paying in rent, but with the added advantage that they would eventually own their own house. Gresswell's profit on the scheme was around £300. He put together a series of similar purchases over the next few years, which were all successful but which also created a financial problem.

The Halifax, which had been providing mortgages for the tenants, found out about the second mortgages and insisted that an amount equivalent to the second mortgage be deposited with the Society in order that it had further security on its loans. He eventually held £5,000 with the Society, which was money that he needed to keep on funding his business. Gresswell came up with a solution and proposed to the Halifax that the security they needed could be achieved by a pool deposit which, as it was highly unlikely that all the mortgages would go into default, need not be anything like the size of the total individual deposits.

The Halifax initially rejected the idea saying that it was against their normal practice. Gresswell, however, knew Denham who was on the Halifax board, and after discussing the pool idea Denham suggested a direct approach to Sir Enoch Hill. To Gresswell's surprise Hill agreed and released £3,000 of the existing deposit money, which was enough to get the house-buying programme rolling again. Denham was impressed by Gresswell's business model and in 1928 the two of them along with two Bradford solicitors set up BPT.

The ready availability of Halifax Building Society funds, often for low value housing with a high geographic concentration in one area, was of undoubted assistance to BPT in its formative years. It is questionable how acceptable this kind of lending, which was effectively providing 100 per cent mortgages, would have been to the Halifax, were it not for the fact that Denham was President of the Society. These more liberal interpretations of building society best practice contrasted sharply with Denham's prudent attitude in discussions with the BSA. Not only does there appear to be dual standards regarding 100 per cent lending but also the whole issue of individual investments greater than £5,000 needs to be seen in perspective.

In 1957 Herbert Newton, a past Chairman of the BSA, commented that on investigating the balance sheets of 22 societies with total assets of £1,000 million the number of accounts with balances greater than £5,000 numbered 2,091 with a total balance was £34 million.

One final view on Denham's integrity is that the more cynical members of the Society's staff, who were there at the time, thought that his desire to hold down mortgage interest rates was purely driven by the BPT business case – if the interest payments were too high their customers would be paying more in mortgage repayments than they used to pay in rent.

Bentley for his part found that he could not satisfy two masters. Many a person would have been satisfied with being General Manager of the Halifax, realising that the politics of wanting to serve as BSA chairman were not worth the risks. The dispute turned out to be essentially a conflict of personalities. A further issue that must have upset Bentley was the appointment to the board in 1955 of Denham's son Jack, who had been an agent for the Society in Bailiff Bridge, an outskirt of the nearby town of Brighouse. This appointment must have smacked of nepotism to Bentley who had served the Society for 40 years without being offered the status of being a board member.

As for the Halifax Building Society it would have been much better for its public image had these matters been resolved behind closed doors, but even so it is difficult to quantify any real long term damage. One final thought on the whole affair is that it would never have happened in Sir Enoch Hill's day – he was President and General Manager and also served as Chairman of the BSA!

5

1956 - 1970

With the premature departure of Fred Bentley in the summer of 1956 Algy Denham had to think who was to replace him as General Manager. As has been already mentioned, Raymond Potter had been brought into the Society in 1951 with an eye to him taking on the top executive position in due course. He was shadowed by Albert Thayre who was seen as the second candidate for the position should anything untoward happen. Both had seen duties in the inspectors' department and at the time of Bentley's resignation they were running their own branches – Potter at Coventry and Thayre at Bournemouth.

At the age of 40 and only having five years' experience at the Society, Potter's appointment to General Manager may well have been seen as a little too premature and risky for the time. So with the prudence that so befitted the organisation, the board appointed two joint General Managers, Raymond Potter and Edwin Beresford. To give further support the executive team was strengthened by making three new positions of Assistant General Manager – Stanley A P Pullin (Mortgages), Alexander O Thomson (Finance) and Albert J Thayre (Staff).

Edwin Beresford cuts the cake at the 1956 Christmas Party.

Beresford first joined the Society at its Huddersfield branch in 1914. After service in a cavalry regiment in the First World War he rejoined the Society in Bradford in 1920 and after various promotions ended up in charge of staff and branches. With over 30 years of experience, and knowing every branch manager, he was obviously considered a safe pair of hands to carry on running the day-to-day operation of the Society. He was generally well liked and, although sometimes a little blusterous, had a pragmatic style of management. This view is supported by an anecdote relating to how one day he filled a branch management vacancy in the Midlands. The story goes that he opened his office door, looked around to see if he could spot a suitable candidate for the job, and on so doing told the individual to pack his bags and get down there.

Sir Raymond Potter at the time of his retirement in 1983.

Potter by contrast was more of an academic - polite, not aggressive, an interesting public speaker and sometimes self-deprecating but with a sense of humour. Coming from the south he often found the industrial Halifax scenery and the harsh Pennine weather depressing. It was said that if these really got him down all he needed to do was take a trip to Todmorden where he would realise that there were people even worse off and he would then return to Halifax in a more contented frame of mind! He took more of an interest in the Society's external relationships and was happy to leave the operational running of the Society to Beresford.

A major issue for both of them during the late 1950s was a greater volatility in interest rates, bank base rate peaking at 7 per cent in 1957 compared with 3 per cent in 1954. The Society, along with the rest of the movement, had to respond to these conditions with mortgage rates peaking at 6 per cent and investors' share rate at 3.5 per cent Legislation also brought about changes, particularly the 1959 House Purchase and Housing Act, which encouraged loans on pre-1919 houses, an area in which the Society had not previously been heavily involved.

The joint General Managers worked well together and in 1960 Beresford retired and Potter was made Chief General Manager, thus finally running the show on his own. Thayre took over most of Beresford's responsibilities being promoted to the position of General Manager along with Pullin, Thomson and George Jennings (General Manager London).

In 1961 Denham died at the age of 76 having completed just short of 40 years as a board member of the Halifax. Ian A D Maclean, who was a

Ian A D Maclean

director of John Crossley and Sons carpet manufactures (based in Halifax), succeeded him as President. In the past there had often been a board representative from the Crossley family and it was Patrick Crossley, who had been the Halifax's first choice back in 1953. Although declining the position himself he suggested Maclean as a suitable board member. Maclean had an engineering background and in the boardroom he was a good decision maker and was also more open to comparing the Society with other organisations and paying the market rate for the job. He also instigated the informal Tuesday evening meeting and dinner prior to the Wednesday board meeting. Unfortunately on a public platform, such as the AGM, he did not appear particularly knowledgeable and would quickly pass on any questions from the floor to Potter or another executive to answer.

The changes that the Society saw during the 1960s were maybe small beer in comparison with those experienced today but nevertheless they were significant for the time. For example:

- ◆ 1963 – for young married couples the joint income of husband and wife could be taken into account when applying for a mortgage.
- ◆ 1963 – the Chief General Manager could approve loans up to £5,000, but all advances greater than £3,500 would still be reported to the board for information.
- ◆ 1964 – discontinue the option of lunar payments for new borrowers.
- ◆ 1964 – investors' interest to be credited half yearly.
- ◆ 1964 – investors' interest to be calculated on a daily basis instead of minimum monthly balance, so as to be more competitive and bring the Society into line with other large societies.
- ◆ 1965 – managers' conferences to become residential, two to be held in the spring and two in the autumn.
- ◆ 1966 – directors' remuneration increased to £35,000 in total. The President was paid £4,000, the Vice President £3,500 and all other directors £2,500.
- ◆ 1966 – assets reach £1 billion.
- ◆ 1968 – new rules for the board to bring it into line with other comparable organisations. Maximum number of directors increased to 18 along with the introduction of executive directors. Any director must resign if all the other directors ask for the resignation.

The most significant change of all was, however, the rapid rate of growth in the Society's business. The post-war growth in assets during the 1950s and 1960s averaged around 13 per cent a year. This was impressive and reflected not only the increasing wealth in post-war Britain but also the general success of the building society movement. Even more impressive was the fact that the Halifax's share of the total assets of the movement went up from 11.8 per cent in 1953 to 15.6 per cent in 1970.

During this period there was major growth of all the larger societies at the expense of the smaller ones. In spite of all these notable growth statistics only one issue really mattered for most people associated with the Society and that was how near the Abbey National was to catching up with the Halifax? Whilst the board could argue that the quality of business, a sound balance sheet and a good deal for the borrower were more important than sheer size there is little doubt that had the Abbey overtaken the Halifax the effect on staff morale, and possibly customer loyalty, would have been disastrous. The fight for market share with the Abbey always seemed to be an unfair one, the Halifax in effect fighting with a self imposed 'hand tied behind the back'. Abbey's heartland was in the much more prosperous south and they were not as concerned as the Halifax with issues like hot money and reserve ratios. They would also usually be offering the BSA recommended investors' interest rates and were not against the paying of introductory commission for investment money. The Abbey's assets were on average around 80 per cent of the Halifax's assets, but appendix 5 shows how much the Halifax had taken its eye off the ball in 1955 and 1956 with the Fred Bentley affair when that figure reached 90 per cent. By 1958, with the resolution of its internal problems and investors' rates that were more competitive there was a return to the status quo of around 80 per cent.

On the investors' side of the business many smaller savers were starting to use the Halifax's class 2 accounts as a poor man's bank account, using a passbook and the branch network as an alternative to a proper bank account with a chequebook. By the 1960s the number of investors accounts as well as the number of transactions per account were both growing at over 10 per cent a year. To accommodate this growth more staff were taken on and more branches were opened. The annual increase in the number of branches between 1953 and 1970 averaged around 4 per cent, which was still less than the increase in the number of transactions.

The Halifax was still very much a northern-based society, but the real potential lay in the south, especially London and the South East. Branches were opened in places such as Guildford and Chelmsford to try and accommodate the needs of customers in the areas where they lived. However, many of these customers were commuters and wanted a branch service in the place where they worked, branches therefore having to be opened in other parts of the city such as Holborn, Kensington, Moorgate and Victoria.

In the early 1960s going into the Society's Commercial Street Halifax branch to pay in money could be quite a time consuming operation. The first task was to try and guess which of the many queues for the different cashiers was moving the fastest. On joining a particular queue, one passed the time by wondering whether to swap to apparently faster moving queues and also thinking why didn't other members of the back office staff, who were clearly visible, stop what they were doing and open up another counter position. Such was the loyalty to the organisation in its birthplace, but this loyalty could not be counted on elsewhere in the country. The days of central queuing and part-time cashiers to cover lunchtime were some way off. The posting of counter sheet transactions to back office ledgers and the balancing of the same was seen as the most important task and many a branch manager could justifiably feel pleased when all his ledgers were up to date and balanced. One could have sympathy with the London branches who, in contrast to the northern branches, were often months behind in posting their transactions and had to rely heavily on relief staff from other branches to get them through to the end of the day. The pressures for them were greater with their lack of experienced staff.

The solution to these problems of growth was to automate the transaction processing. Burroughs direct accounting machines had been installed as far back as 1955 but these were no more than semi-intelligent printers. In June 1963 a resolution was placed before the board recommending the installation of a computer. The business case was based upon savings in staff, overtime and branch premises with English Electric, Honeywell, IBM, ICT and NCR being asked to make proposals. A task force was set up under the leadership of Thomson as it was standard practice in those days to give responsibility, for what was regarded as a glorified adding machine, to a company's Chief Accountant. Thomson qualified as a Scottish Accountant and worked for Deloitte, Plender and Griffiths of London prior to joining the Society in 1949. There was a feeling that his Scottish rather than English qualifications prevented him from making progress to the top of the accountancy firm and this maybe influenced his move to the Society. He was a hardworking individual who commanded the respect of Potter, and in certain ways he saw himself as Potter's deputy ahead of Thayre. At a manager's conference when Potter got called away on urgent BSA business it was Thomson rather than Thayre who took over and conducted the summing up session. Thomson led the project to install the computer in typical Halifax fashion ensuring that everything must be done correctly so that the Society's administrative reputation would not be jeopardised.

IBM won the contract to supply the computer system and work started on building a new multi-storey office block in Trinity Road, Halifax to house the machine and its associated staff. Delivery of the machine was fixed for early 1967 when the Trinity Road building would be complete and the Society's own systems analysts and programmers would have developed the initial software. This was not a project to be rushed and as Thomson explained in a *Halifax Courier* article in 1965, 'a computer is not like a second hand car or a long-playing record. You just don't walk into a shop and buy it'.

Although the Halifax was one of the first three companies in Yorkshire to install IBM's latest System 360 machine they were not the first to use computers in Calderdale. This claim went to, of all firms, Thornbers poultry firm of Mytholmroyd. Testing of the first programmes entailed using machines in IBM locations in London and latterly at National Provincial bank in Bradford. Progress of other installations was keenly followed and concern was expressed at board level when Martins bank cancelled an order for three IBM machines and decided instead to order machines from NCR. The Society asked IBM to give written confirmation that the machine it had ordered, a System 360 model 40 with 64k of memory, would have sufficient capacity to perform the Society's task. Because of concerns over capacity the machine that was eventually delivered in 1967 had 128K of memory and cost £330,794. Potter reported back to staff in the pages of

Installation of Halifax Building Socieites new computer,
as reported in the Weekly Courier & Guardian, March 12, 1965.

(Courtesy of Halifax Courier)

Round the Table with his usual wit quoting 'the animal concerned has already been put into its new cage in Halifax'. In February 1968 he quoted: 'To date, our friend the computer is proving a very healthy infant and, from this end, we are well pleased with the results achieved at this stage'. It was left to Calum Macaskill to report more factually in September 1968 on the plans to have all investors' accounts converted by November 1969 and borrowers' accounts by mid 1970, which would be well ahead of 'decimalisation day' in February 1971.

All the software was written in-house by the Society's own staff in IBM Assembler language. Sheets of transactions were posted in by the branches to Head Office where they were converted onto punched cards for feeding into the computer. Reports were produced and posted back to the branches confirming the transactions that had been posted, along with any errors that may have been encountered. At the end of the year the computer posted the relevant interest transaction and produced two copies of all the transactions posted for an individual account. One copy was sent to the branch, which in effect replaced their previous ledger sheets, and the other formed a statement that was sent to the customer for information and also as a valuable audit check on what the Society had posted for that customer. The computerisation of the Society's accounts heralded a fundamental shift in its administration, in that the accounts were now held centrally rather than at the branch, albeit that the branch was still responsible for all input to these accounts. The branch could request a print out of information held by the computer for any customer for the current year, but they would have to wait until at least the next day's post to receive it.

The removal of a branch's accounting records was seen as one of the main drawbacks of what was otherwise considered as a very successful application of the new computer. A high tech solution was available, this being to install a terminal in all the branches such that they could again have immediate access to all their accounts. In order to test this concept it was decided to install a terminal in the Head Office staff department so that they could access and update sensitive personnel data (such as salaries!) without the need to involve computer staff who would have to handle printouts containing this data. Staff department was seen as extremely important and powerful, mainly because of Thayre's interest in people and personnel matters.

The staff online IBM 2740 terminal

The board approved a paper in February 1968 to install the 'staff online system', the cost being £11,000 for a new disk drive to hold the staff file and £10,000 for a single terminal linked to the computer. Delivery lead-time for this equipment was 18 months and the in-house developed software could only be tested once this equipment had been installed. The IBM 2740 terminal ordered was similar to the console on the main computer having keyboard input with an IBM 'golfball' printing onto continuous stationery. There were no VDU monitors until the early 1970s and mechanical malfunctioning of the main console often caused the whole computer system to crash. Staff department were reassured by the fact that their disk was of a removable variety that could be locked away when the terminal system was not operational thus preventing unauthorised access to their sensitive data. They gave no consideration to the fact that this disk was backed up to magnetic tape and this data was easily accessible to programmers and operators alike – this thinking was indeed naïve even for 1969!

In parallel with the development of the staff online system a board paper was being prepared outlining the business case for a national branch teleprocessing system. This paper was approved by the board in

In the absence of Raymond Potter, who was on holiday, Alexander Thomson (right) makes the retirement presentation to Donald Bromley, head office solicitor, with John Spalding looking on.

September 1969 and argued a business case based on improved branch and customer service rather than any particular cost savings.

Management information was also the responsibility of Thomson and his finance department who had to collate daily return information from all the branches to understand what the total business picture was for the Society. Of particular importance was the net inflow situation for the Society, which in the end dictated how much lending could be performed. Thomson could also claim to be the first in-house accountant to prepare the annual report and accounts, this previously being performed by Harry Riley, a local firm of accountants.

He also performed the role of secretary by taking the minutes of board meetings, a task he performed by writing copious notes in red ink. Unfortunately these notes were unintelligible to most people including Thomson himself. The exception to this was Thomson's secretary Mary Farrar, who over the years had developed the requisite deciphering skills. He was an integral member of the senior team underneath Potter, which saw the Society through the successful years of the late 1950s and 1960s. He retired in June 1970 from his position as General Manager but remained on the board as a non-executive director. He was one of the first three post-war executives to be invited onto the board in 1968, the other two being Potter the Chief General Manager and Thayre, General

Manager. On his retirement there was another restructuring of the executive as follows:

Albert Thayre	Deputy Chief General Manager
Calum Macaskill	General Manager Computer Department
Gordon Sykes	General Manager Staff
Richard Wheway	General Manager Finance
John Spalding	General Manager Legal.

The joke went that Thomson was so hard working that he had to be replaced by four other General Managers. Thayre was regarded by many staff as the most visible and senior of the executive. He had a remarkable skill in people management, never forgetting a face or a name and insisting on interviewing every employee who started with the Society before they got their letter of employment. This was no mean feat when one realises that the Society had nearly 150 branches and meant that new branch staff, once the local manager had approved them, had to travel the length and breadth of the country to meet Thayre in Halifax.

Albert J Thayre

He gained popularity with the workforce by going out of his way to talk to them, it being just as likely to see him chatting to people in the kitchen as it was in the board room. Often after having listened to him for 20 or 30 minutes it was difficult to remember exactly what he had said. An observation of Thayre by Ronnie Parkinson (late Head Office 'lifer') was that 'if he could not think of anything to say he kept on talking until something came into his head'. Amongst his outside interests he was involved with Bradford University where he became Pro-Chancellor in 1969 and worked with Harold Wilson, who was then the University's Chancellor

The culture of the Society was to offer lifetime employment and promote staff from within the organisation to management positions. The rare exception to this was the external recruitment of a few specialists such as accountants and solicitors. The Society had a provincial attitude and on visiting just about any branch in the country one was greeted by a manager who invariably had a Yorkshire accent. However, the policy worked well and undoubtedly contributed to the success of the Society, but had disadvantages including the risk of being out of line with regard to the remuneration of the more senior or specialist jobs.

In 1968 a graduate started on a salary of £800 knew that had they become a teacher they would have been paid £1,000. There were constant battles in those early years trying to get something close to market rate for what was considered specialist computer skills. Management thought the computer staff should be on a similar pay scale to branch personnel and indeed there was a belief that once the job of programming the computer was completed, they would have to be redeployed back into the branch organisation. With a headcount of less than 20 computer development staff no one could envisage the thousands of IT personnel employed at the turn of the century.

Things had started to change back in 1965 when Denis Macnaught, who was Thomson's deputy, was successful in applying for the job of General Manager designate of the Huddersfield Building Society. Macnaught's new salary with the Huddersfield was in excess of anything the Halifax was paying its own executives, with the exception of Potter. On being questioned by senior staff at Head Office, who felt that they were also under-paid, Thayre was somewhat dismissive about the situation. He stated that 'the Huddersfield Building Society was no bigger than our own Huddersfield branch and its assets were only equivalent to one day's growth of our own'. Be that as it may, a point had been made by Macnaught's departure that instigated a change, albeit a slow one, to the remuneration of the Society's staff. Neither Potter nor Thayre were particularly driven by financial reward and salary increases for off scale staff were seen as something which were handed out on a personal basis and the recipients should be duly grateful.

Macnaught's departure also highlighted a weakness in Thomson's

Portrait of Algernon Denham President 1945 – 1961

(*Courtesy of HBOS plc*)

The HOME OWNER

The popular members' magazine Home Owner featured The Howroyde
in Barkisland, Halifax in January 1957

Ian Maclean listening to Albert Thayre during a lunch held at the
Saddlers Hall, London, 1973

(*Courtesy of HBOS plc*)

An old print of Ramsden's brewery which stood on the site now occupied by the Halifax head office

The Halifax new head office contrasts with the older buildings in the town centre

Sir Raymond and Lady Potter with their eldest son and daughter, after Sir Raymond's investiture at Buckingham Palace in 1978

Staff from London Hanover Square, Preston Fishergate and York Davygate
at the last staff dance in October 1983

Leeds Commercial Street staff promoting Cardcash during open evenings held in September 1984.

management style, this being to allocate tasks to individuals without any sense of putting them into the total picture or involving them as a team. He jealously protected his relationship with other board members and he could be described as adopting a divide and conquer style of management. With Macnaught gone, the Society needed a person to take over from Thomson when he retired in 1970. The Society advertised on the open market and secured the services of a K C Stephenson who had previously been with the pig marketing board. Stephenson came in December 1965 but was gone by following summer due to the fact that he could not get on with Thomson. This left the Society in a potentially embarrassing situation in the fact that they did not want to advertise the same position again so soon after it had been supposedly filled. The situation was resolved when Gordon Hunter, who was a board member and Vice President, recommended a contact of his from Coopers Lybrand in Leeds called Richard Wheway, who was offered and accepted the position of Assistant General Manager of finance in January 1967.

As the 1960s came to a close the Society had grown and changed impressively from the one that celebrated its 100th anniversary in 1953. Board structure and number of directors had changed but interestingly their remuneration was not significantly out of line with that paid today when compared on the basis of total asset size. This was, however, prior to Thatcherism and many directors could well have been paying income tax at the top rate of 18s 6d in the pound (although there was a two ninths earned income allowance)! Significant changes had taken place in the Society's executive, assets had increased seven-fold, the number of branches had doubled and a computer had been installed. In 1953 investors, who in the main were regular savers, were true shareholders looking forward to their annual dividend as a payout from the profits of the Society. By 1970 an ever-increasing proportion of the Society's resources were being spent on servicing investors with active accounts and on operating a quota system to ration mortgages.

6

THE 1970s

Many members of staff knew and respected Raymond Potter but absolutely everybody knew and had met Albert Thayre. At the start of the 1970s Thayre was deputy to Potter the Chief General Manager. When Potter became Chairman on 1 December 1974 Thayre stepped up to be Chief General Manager, a position he held until he retired in 1982. Whatever titles they held the Potter/Thayre double act seemed to work extremely well.

Thayre's forte was people and he spent most of his waking hours communicating with them. He started first thing in the morning on his way into Head Office from his home in Northowram, when he would eagerly look out for members of staff waiting at bus stops to whom he could give a lift into work – and talk to them at the same time. Certain young lads, on seeing Thayre's Rover car, would hide out of sight in order that they could continue their more everyday conversation of football, girls and beer on their journey into work. One morning Thayre, who already had a car full of Halifax staff, stopped at a bus stop where he had spotted other staff to explain to them why he could not offer them a lift on this particular day.

Before he went home in an evening he would invariably do a tour of head office to see who was still at work. As this was after six o'clock, and in those days most staff went home on the stroke of quarter past five, the people he came across were usually cleaners, security staff, electricians, joiners or computer staff either working late or on shifts. No matter who they were they would be treated to a discourse on the day's business as seen through Thayre's eyes. At managers' conferences Thayre was as likely to be seen thanking the hotel staff for their efforts as he was talking to employees of the Halifax.

There are many stories relating to Thayre but the following comments he made at the 1975 AGM typify the man and his beliefs, and show how he was ahead of the game when it came to market research. He told of how he had helped an old man put up his umbrella in the wind and rain outside the Halifax's Oxford branch. 'Did they treat you well in the branch?' Thayre had enquired. 'Yes very well and I have been coming here for 50 years', answered the old man. Thayre's written communications, like his verbal ones, could be lengthy. In the September 1978 edition of *Round the Table*, Thayre reported on his recent holiday in Italy and also his wartime service in Florence, where 'incidentally I was awarded my MBE'. He eventually concludes with 'if you wonder why I have written all this it is perhaps just to make the point in a new way that nothing matters more than caring about people'.

In the October 1977 edition of *Round the Table*, Thayre relishes relating a tale of how Harry Jagger, the ex Bristol district manager, had been invited to a party by two customers who were celebrating making the final repayment of their mortgage loan. The loan, which was of an unusual nature, had been arranged by Jagger after a personal interview with the couple and was made after they had been turned down by several other societies. A further example of Thayre's true commitment to his job is found in the first *Round the Table* of 1976 where he tells his readers that he is drafting his comments 'within an hour of having heralded in the New Year'.

There was, however, a feeling that Thayre was the right man for the job, but had arrived at the wrong time. He embodied the founding principles of the Halifax and the building society movement but during the 1970s these basic beliefs were being challenged by external economic

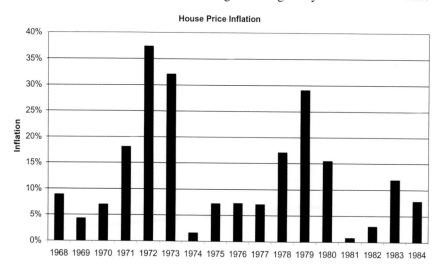

House Price Inflation

factors. House prices rose steadily throughout the 1950s and 1960s but in general the rises were modest and tracked the increases in average earnings. However, during the 1970s house prices demonstrated a marked volatility, with a major boom in 1972/1973 with annual house price inflation of well over 30 per cent followed by a similar boom in 1979.

These booms were a consequence of many factors including the post-war baby boom requiring their own household, the historically low ratio of house prices to earnings and significant increases in real personal disposable income. The 1970s were pre Margaret Thatcher with Heath, Wilson and Callaghan all failing to control strong trade union demands for large pay settlements, leading to inflation that averaged over 15 per cent per annum for several years and peaked at 24 per cent in 1975 (see appendix 6). Interest rates were used as a major weapon in trying to combat inflation and bank rate reached 12 per cent or over in all the years from 1973 to 1980, peaking at 17 per cent in 1979 (see appendix 7). Building society rates tracked this upward trend until in May 1973, when the mortgage rate was to be increased from 9.5 per cent to 10 per cent, the government stepped in feeling that double-digit mortgage rates would be politically unacceptable to the electorate. A 0.5 per cent subsidy was granted to borrowers for a period of three months by which time it was hoped that the crisis would be over and interest rates would be on their way down. This was something of a forlorn hope and after the three months had elapsed rates were increased to 10 per cent and later on in the year to 11 per cent. Mortgage rates remained at or around 11 per cent for the rest of the 1970s, actually peaking at 15 per cent in 1979 (see appendix 9).

Sympathy had traditionally been with the building society borrower, trying to make their lot in life as easy as possible. With these unprecedented high interest rates there was real concern as to whether borrowers would be able to keep up their repayments. Closer examination of the situation leads to the view that maybe this sympathy was misplaced. Referring again to appendix 9 it can be seen that during the 1950s and 1960s the mortgage rate always exceeded the rate of inflation, which was kept below 5 per cent. It should be noted, however, that up to 1974, income tax relief was given for the interest on the full amount of any loan. After 1974 the relief was limited to the interest on a maximum loan of

£25,000 but this amount was sufficient for the vast majority of house purchases. So for taxpayers, especially higher rate taxpayers, there was substantial tax relief on their interest payments. Even for non-taxpayers the introduction of the option mortgage scheme in 1969 meant that all borrowers were in effect getting at least a 30 per cent reduction in their interest rate.

During the 1970s the mortgage rate, even before any tax relief, was usually below the rate of inflation and well below the rate of house price inflation during the two boom periods. These facts were not lost on the British public who now realised that investing in residential property and taking out as large a mortgage as possible was an excellent hedge against inflation and one of the best investments available. During 1972 and 1973 the market was characterised by hysteria with the belief that prices would continue rising at a rate out of all proportion to earnings or the rate of increase of prices generally. The boom of 1972 and 1973 was followed by the bust of 1974 to 1977, when real house prices increased modestly in absolute terms but decreased significantly when taking inflation into account. Buying a property with the aid of a building society mortgage was still an excellent decision for most people and the 1970s heralded the start of a new era where speculation encouraged borrowers not only to buy a home for their needs but to also invest heavily in the property market.

The benefits to the borrower during the 1970s were matched by the losses experienced by the building society investor. Appendix 8 shows how building society investment interest had roughly kept pace with inflation during the 1950s and 1960s. During the 1970s, however, even with interest rates peaking at 10.5 per cent the investor was losing out heavily when inflation was taken into account. Investors who once were willing to put their money in a building society share account for safe keeping were now much more interested in chasing accounts offering the highest interest rates. In the mid 1970s new term share and monthly savings accounts were introduced both offering a premium on the interest being paid on the ordinary share account. It was not long before these accounts were bringing in the lion's share of all new money, there being precious little of this about. As had been the case in the past the Halifax fared better than many of its competitors in these difficult times and at its

1974 AGM it reported that it had not experienced an outflow in any month, which was in contrast to many other societies and the movement as a whole.

At its 1975 AGM it reported that interest rates had remained the same at well below the rate of inflation for the last 19 months. It commented that 'people argue there is no point in saving with an inflation rate of 20%' and a question from the floor asked for an index linked savings product. There was a very real fear that Britain was heading towards being a South American, high inflation type of economy. Building society leaders, including Potter and Thayre, talked about little else other than the evils of inflation, but the root cause of the problem and its solution were out of their control.

The Halifax's encouragement of thrift, which had been its guiding principle for over 120 years, was now very difficult to justify. Thayre, more than anyone, had difficulty in coming to terms with this new turbulent economy. His discussion groups, that he held at Head Office and out in the branch network for junior off-scale staff, only had one topic of conversation. Whilst at a manager's conference in Sheffield in 1976 the news came through that bank base rate had just been increased to 15 per cent. Thayre was so taken aback by this news that he suggested the assembled group of managers should bow their heads and take a minute out for silent prayer!

Quotas for new mortgage business were still in operation for most of the 1970s. The problem of raising adequate funds was mentioned at the Society's 1970 AGM with Potter raising the issue again at the 1979 AGM saying that as a solution he was opposed to raising funds on the money market. A 0.25 per cent differential was introduced on endowment mortgages in 1973, as these mortgages did not provide any capital repayment until the end of their term. In 1977 differential rates were introduced with larger mortgage loans attracting a higher rate of interest. This was seen as a way of directing funds to borrowers with more modest requirements and would help in the rationing of funds.

Thayre liked to be in control and to be seen to be in control of the organisation. When it came to salary increases for off-scale members of staff it was Thayre who decided who got what. He was also increasingly aware of the power base of the people in charge of the computer system. Traditionally he could move managers from one administrative area to another but specialist knowledge, and not just man management skills, was required for the senior positions in the computer department. The initial computerisation of the Society's accounts had been very successful, but in general it had been a matter of automating the previous manual system. A second phase was now taking place that involved re-examining all the Society's administration but with the knowledge of the computer's capabilities. The IBM 3980 Bank Teleprocessing System, which had received board approval in 1969, started to be installed in branches in 1971. Data keyed into these terminals by the branch was still processed in batch mode overnight, but at least it was processed a day earlier than when branches had to post their counter sheets to Head Office. This terminal system also allowed account enquiries, thus giving back to branches the access that had been taken away by the first phase of computerisation. Extra functionality was provided by three new investor's enquiries:

BAL - give an up-to-date balance of an account

REP - give a repayment amount for an account including up to
date interest

WPB - Write up Pass Book with all Not In Book (NIB) transactions

Fred Dawson, Richard Westwood and Mike Whitehouse who were key people in developing the software for the IBM 3980 terminal system.

The technical specification of the terminal system was minimal in comparison with today's standards eg a 1,200 baud line supporting as many as 32 terminals. Nevertheless by cutting down the message formats to the absolute minimum, one terminal would support the average branch's business, the larger branches such as Halifax and Huddersfield having as many as four terminals.

Magnetic tapes were supplied by all the major clearing banks which contained details of bank standing orders and credits, thus allowing this data to be processed centrally rather than branches having to laboriously key the data from information supplied on paper by the banks. Internal standing orders were introduced allowing customers to pay their mortgage and investment subscriptions from a savings account automatically. Wherever possible automated transaction processing was implemented to reduce the Society's administrative workload. A further development of this philosophy was the introduction of the Society's first ATM, an IBM 3614, in July 1978. This pilot exercise in Halifax was extended to Bradford, Huddersfield and Sheffield in 1979, cards initially being offered to the limited number of deposit cheque account (DCA[1]) holders. Calum Macaskill had to champion the cause of ATMs at executive and board level, with Thayre exhibiting his usual caution, openly stating that the Society must be careful not to tread on the feet of the banks.

One project that started in the early 1970s to automate the general ledger turned into a complete rewrite of all the Society's accounting system. Initially called the 1974 Rationalised Administration System (RAS) it ended up as the Revised Accounting System (still RAS) but the implementation was put back to the Society's 1976 year end – 31 January 1977. Mike Whitehouse, who at the time RAS was implemented had become Controller Computer Systems and Services, very much saw RAS as his baby. Whitehouse later commented that it's never a good idea to use a date in the name of any new computer system! Thayre's observation about RAS was that 'at a stroke you have taken away the last remaining knowledge I have of the Society's accounting systems'. A computer maintained branch general ledger, a streamlining of the previous vast number of different counter sheets, allowing foreign branch transactions

---

[1] *The deposit cheque account was commonly referred to as DCA by both staff and customers*

72

(ie, a transaction for an account not held at the processing branch) and automating account transfers between branches were some of the most significant changes.

RAS remains the Society's accounting system to this day and it took the clearing banks decades to catch up and implement similar features such as the acceptance of foreign branch transactions. All of RAS was developed by the Society's own computer staff continuing the belief that the main accounting systems needed to be developed 'in house'. Packaged solutions were unable to cope with the scale of the Society's operation and provided too limited functionality.

As the decade drew to a close an £11.25 million contract was signed with Philips Business systems for a PTS 6000 terminal system that provided VDU screens and cashier terminals capable of automatically updating passbooks. The PTS 6000 was specially developed for financial institutions and did not come cheap in comparison with today's consumer PC equipment, with an 11 inch monochrome VDU costing £900, a keyboard £300 and the passbook printer £1,300. Nevertheless the system proved to be cost effective in reducing the branch administration as well as improving customer service. At the same time the Abbey National and the Nationwide were also implementing similar cashier terminal systems, all of these developments being years in advance of anything the major clearing banks were installing.

Throughout the 1960s and early 1970s IBM were a very dominant supplier and it was expected that if you had an IBM central processor you would buy all of your other computer equipment from them. The feeling was that there would be no connectivity or interface problems if all of your equipment came from the same supplier and the golden rule for computer managers was 'you never get sacked for buying from IBM'. However, towards the end of the 1970s the Society was buying most of its equipment from other suppliers such as Amdahl, Memorex and Philips because of significant cost savings coupled with better performance and reliability.

Like a true 'cut and thrust' American company, IBM did not take this loss of business lying down and used just about every trick in the book to try and regain it. In 1979 Eddie Nixon, chairman of IBM UK, visited

Potter at the Society's London flat with the intention of discrediting the judgment of the Society's IT management. To his credit Potter politely listened to what Nixon had to say, offered him another cup of tea and then sent him on his way with a clear impression that the Society's board were quite happy to let technical decisions be made by the organisation's technical staff. Nixon's actions were never repeated and IBM realised they had made a fundamental error of judgment which cost them dearly in the years ahead. This situation of total trust in the judgment and integrity of the Society's IT department lasted until the early 1990s when new outside board and executive personnel felt the need to be involved with IT suppliers and consultants at a technical level.

As in previous decades the Society assisted smaller societies if they were in trouble – eg the Derbyshire in 1971 following a run on its funds after the financial collapse of Rolls Royce, and the Wakefield in 1976 following financial irregularities by its Chief Executive. In the case of the Derbyshire, the Halifax provided a loan of £2 million in order to improve its liquidity. John Spalding, the Head Office solicitor, drove down the M1 with a cheque but before he had reached his destination the news had got out that the mighty Halifax was supporting the Derbyshire. This news alone put a halt to the run on the Derbyshire with the vast majority of the withdrawn funds being paid back in, and the Halifax loan itself was repaid within two months. The cost and risk of the loan was minimal and was far outweighed by the excellent PR the Society obtained.

In 1977 Thayre restructured the branch network into 12 regions each with its own Regional Manager. With increasing centralisation of product development, marketing and, above all, administration, the power and responsibility of the branch network was decreasing such that the role of the regions was never easily understood. Certain aspects of sales monitoring, personnel and premises management were, however, devolved to the regions and this extra regional management layer provided further career opportunities for branch personnel.

Conferences and social events started to be held on a regional basis but even at the end of the decade the annual staff dance was still being held centrally at the Victoria Hall in Halifax, although the frequency with which staff members were invited had been reduced. Edwin Harper and his band from Bridlington helped to provide musical entertainment, his fee being credited directly to his mortgage account!

Further changes in the area of employee relations came about in 1978 when the Society signed a recognition agreement with the Halifax Staff Association. John Simmons from the Plymouth branch was the driving force behind its creation and his actions were seen as a brave challenge to the Society's management, and Thayre in particular. Its formation was undoubtedly brought about by the Society's conservative approach to wage settlements and their desire to stick rigidly to the many government guidelines imposed during the 1970s.

Albert J Thayre presents a gold watch to Edwin Harper, the orchestra leader, after 20 years service at the Society's staff dance.

Changes of personnel at board and executive level continued to follow the Halifax tradition of being well thought out and non-radical. At the 1971 AGM the total fee for the 13 board directors was increased to £60,000. Mention was made of the rules that applied prior to 1944 - these allowed fees of 250 guineas per £1 million of assets which in 1971 terms would have equated to fees of greater than £500,000. Potter commented

that the rules had been rightly changed as the Society had grown. Fred Bentley had also gone from the board by the time of this AGM, little or no mention ever being made of his retirement.

In 1973 the term President was replaced with Chairman and new rules forced all directors to retire at the age of 70 but with the option that they could then be re-elected. Also a third of the board had to retire every year and the power was given to create local and regional boards. This power was used in 1974 when the London board was set up under the chairmanship of Sir James Whitaker with one of the first co-opted members being Dick Hornby. Although the London board tended to be a discussion rather than a decision making forum, it proved extremely useful as a means of evaluating potential full board members and was obviously much more attractive to London based people in terms of time commitment.

At the end of 1974, Maclean retired noting that in his $13^{1}/_{2}$ years as Chairman he had never had to take a vote. Potter succeeded him and in the minor realignment of responsibilities Nigel Watson was made a General Manager, reflecting the growing importance of marketing within the organisation.

Potter also became Chairman of the BSA in 1975, this being a position for which he was eminently suited and an appointment that finally put an end to any rift between the Halifax and its trade body. During his time in office there was much dialogue with the government, not only on the major problem of inflation, but also on the cutbacks in local authority lending. It was also the start of an era when it was becoming increasingly difficult to obtain members' agreements on interest rate undertakings.

In 1978 Potter received a knighthood for his undoubted contribution to the Halifax and the building society industry at large. In the same year the board started to meet just once a month on the third Wednesday – thus acknowledging the fact that all the day-to-day decisions were the responsibility of the executive and also recognising the problem of attracting suitable non-executives to attend meetings in Halifax. Of all these considerable changes the most unusual was the move of Potter from being Chief General Manager to that of Chairman of the board – not since the days of Sir Enoch Hill had one person taken this progression. The reason for this move was that the board would only allow Potter his wish to become Chairman of the BSA as long as he also relinquished his role of being the Society's Chief Executive. The board were obviously still mindful of the circumstances that had led up to the 'Fred Bentley affair'.

The expanding business of the Society necessitated a need for further office accommodation. Macaskill often stated that the Society was very good at building new offices and all of them were located in Halifax. The loyalty the Society showed to its birthplace was, however, beneficial to both parties. Wealth generated by its presence in the town cannot be disputed and in return neither can the provision of an adaptable, educated and stable workforce. Various post-war extensions to Permanent Buildings and the commissioning of the new computer building in Trinity Road still did not provide enough office space.

The new Head Office building from Commercial Street

Following the purchase in 1967 of the old Ramsden's brewery site, which was next to the computer building, a working team was set up to provide the input specification of a new Head Office for the architects, Building Design Partnership. Up to this point the architects for most of the Society's buildings in Halifax had been the local firm Clement Williams, but it was decided that the new building was of such size and importance that a well-known national firm of architects should be commissioned.

The first purpose of the building was to provide a prestigious and impressive Head Office building with appropriate facilities for the board and executive. The second requirement was to accommodate the huge mortgage offer and repayment process that was based in Halifax. Central to this later requirement was the need for a strong room for the storage of all the Society's mortgage deeds and traditionally such rooms had always been located underground in a safe basement. This same thinking was applied to the design specification for the new building necessitating the blasting out of rock going down to a depth of 50 feet. The deeds and associated correspondence files were to be transported by automatic conveyors to the working departments in the general office on the third floor, which was elevated and supported by four pylons situated at the corners of the site. Above the third floor was to be a fourth that would accommodate the board and executive.

The building contractor was Laings with the contract for the £1.6 million automated deed and correspondence systems (initially called Conserv-a-trieve) going to Roneo Ltd which in turn was guaranteed by Vickers Ltd and was designed by Supreme Manufacturing Inc of Brooklyn New York. This automated store was ahead of its time and the venture was seen as uncharacteristically risky for the Society. The cost of the building with fittings was around £10 million, and staff occupied it in 1973 with Conserv-a-trieve being commissioned a year later. The Queen made a visit in the same year on 13 November 1974.

The 1970s was a period of significant branch development with the number nearly doubling to just short of 400 by the end of the decade. Many of these new outlets, termed local branches, were relatively small and came under the overall management of a nearby main branch.

Similarly the number of the Society's agencies grew from 800 to over 1400. This expansion of the Society's retail outlets was one of the main ways of attracting new investment funds. Assets grew at a faster rate than in any period since the war, but inflation made a significant contribution to this growth. Assets of £1 billion were reached in 1966 and £2 billion in 1971, the latter milestone being recognised by giving an extra month's salary to all staff. The first milestone unfortunately occurred in a period of Harold Wilson's enforced government pay restraint. There was a modest increase in the Society's share of the total movement's assets, but ground was lost to the Abbey. They ended the decade at 82 per cent of the size of the Halifax, mainly due to more aggressive premier investment product pricing along with the paying of introductory commission. All in all the 1970s was a period of increasing change and challenge to which the Society responded well.

7

1980 – 1986

The Society was like a snowball growing all the time. When it reached £10 billion assets in January 1981 the achievement was recognised by the payment of another bonus to all staff. The organisation's culture was slowly changing - the last subsidised staff holiday took place in 1984 along with the last Halifax Staff Function in the same year. The final edition (number 169) of *Round the Table* was published in 1986.

After over 30 years with the Society, Albert Thayre retired in May 1982 and was succeeded by John Spalding, a solicitor who had been recruited from Hampshire County Council in 1962 to fill a position advertised by the Halifax as 'Assistant Solicitor with Prospects'. Spalding was not without humour and had a management style that was direct, firm and decisive, as is illustrated by a conversation he had with Mike Whitehouse

shortly after he had been promoted to Secretary with responsibility for BIS (Business Information Systems). Spalding wanted Whitehouse to move office to the executive fourth floor but Whitehouse explained that he preferred to be with his troops, in the adjacent Trinity Road building, leading them from the front. Spalding noted his request but explained that he was a five star general whilst Whitehouse was a one star general and he expected to see Whitehouse in his new office on Monday morning - and so it was.

John Spalding, Chief General Manager 1982

Under his Chief General Manager position Spalding created three deputies – Calum Macaskill (marketing and operations), Nigel Watson (premises and personnel) and Richard Wheway (finance and Europe). A year later in the May of 1983 Sir Raymond Potter retired and was succeeded as Chairman by Richard (Dick) Hornby, an intelligent and charismatic individual who was easy to get on with and who had great respect for the Society.

Hornby had joined the London board of the Halifax in 1974, joining the main board two years later and becoming Vice Chairman in 1981. Educated at Oxford he had had a career with the advertising agency J Walter Thompson and was also the Conservative MP for Tonbridge, acting as Parliamentary Under Secretary of State in the Commonwealth Office from 1963 to 1964. He was willing to let the Society's executive run the day-to-day operational business with the board keeping a watching brief along with input on major strategic issues. Thus the Potter/Thayre era came to a close with a smooth transfer of power to the new incumbents. In typical Halifax fashion these new leaders, who were originally brought in from careers outside, were given time to learn the ropes and show their abilities prior to being promoted to running the business.

The challenge associated with being the largest player in any business is to retain that position in spite of your competitors' efforts to try and catch up. So it was with the Halifax in the building society movement and it was to its credit that it had gradually increased its share of the market over the years, more or less retaining its lead over the other larger societies. This had been

Richard Hornby on his retirement as chairman 1990

achieved by developing a large and loyal customer base supported by a good branch network, which focused on administrative excellence and customer service. In spite of its size and efficient administration, its large franchise of investors with relatively small balances meant that its management expense ratio was much the same as the rest of the movement. Competing on interest rates was therefore not an option, as the rest of the movement would follow any lead from the Halifax. The BSA interest rate undertaking could therefore be seen as helpful to the Halifax's competitive position.

One area where the Halifax did, however, have a lead, and one which was not easily followed, was the provision of an ATM service. The Society had already implemented a pilot ATM service using six IBM 3624 ATMs in the lobbies of branches in Halifax, Bradford, Huddersfield and Sheffield, which was made available to 11,000 deposit cheque account customers. In spite of the limited nature of this service the Society's computer staff had developed their own software system whereby any withdrawal, whether it be through the ATM or over the counter, was immediately debited against a customer's account (real time processing). This was in contrast to many of the banks' systems but was essential for a building society where the regulation did not allow savers to have a negative balance or overdraft facility.

Valuable experience was also obtained on the mechanical frailties of the IBM 3624 ATMs, particularly in the printing of statement cards and the dispensing of old bank notes.

In July 1983 the Society launched 'Cardcash' a new non-passbook account that provided a plastic card that could be used in ATMs or at branch or agency counters. Cardcash customers received regular statements (similar to a cheque account) as well as being paid a competitive rate of interest. Within six months 100 Philips ATMs were to be installed through the walls of the Society's larger branches, these machines actually being manufactured by Diebold in the USA but incorporating a British De La Rue note dispenser. The Cardcash product had been well thought out strategically and was designed as a way of moving customers with high transaction activity away from the counter and the use of passbooks. From the outset the product was functionally rich allowing for statement requests, deposits, balance requests as well as cash dispensing.

The ATM was treated as another terminal on the Philips PTS 6000 system, which by now had been rolled out to all front office counter positions as well as some of the larger agencies. Branch staff could balance the ATM, take facilities out and interrogate error logs – all these functions being handled centrally in Halifax when the branch was closed. The Society was unique in getting the branch to 'own' the ATM - they loaded it with cash and replacement statement rolls, they cleaned it and performed daily tests on each of the functions and they were also at the front line in sorting out any problems with the machines. In contrast most other ATMs that were being installed by other financial institutions were serviced and loaded with cash by third party companies. This Halifax approach of branches being responsible for their own ATMs paid dividends not only in higher availability but also in the branch identifying with the Cardcash product. In the autumn 1983 edition of *Viewpoint*, the then business newspaper of the Society, Eddie Shoebridge, assistant manager at Halifax branch (which had the first through the wall ATM), reported:

> … the Cardcash product can be promoted with pride, satisfaction and confidence. For the first time ever a building society has developed an account which cannot be copied by others in the industry overnight nor possibly within 12-18 months.

Shoebridge went on to report on promotional open evenings with wine and advice, female staff going round town with carrier bags, balloons, badges and leaflets and also the 'fantastic' public response to the product. Other branches emulated this enthusiasm for the Cardcash product as their ATMs were installed. Shoebridge's predications on the industry's inability to copy Cardcash came true in the case of the Abbey who had to delay the introduction of their first ATM by 12 months whilst their new packaged ATM software was modified to interface with their main accounting files.

Other larger societies did install a few ATMs but none of them copied the Cardcash concept of a statement-based account. Most merely provided ATM access to existing passbook accounts and therefore did not encourage customers to move away from the branch counter. Enthusiastic

Lyminton's branch manager Steven Williams invited Lord Shackleton (son of the famous Antartic explorer) to open their Cashcard machine.

support for Cardcash was provided by premises department who had to grapple with local planning permission problems and marketing division whose support for the product including the well remembered 'Easy Like Sunday Morning' TV commercial. The Society was onto a winner and it made no sense to join either the Matrix or Link shared ATM networks that would have allowed other societies access to the large number of machines that the Halifax had installed. By August 1985 a total of 350 Halifax ATMs were in place and extra functionality had been developed to allow for bill payments and funds transfers. The opening of the one millionth Cardcash account in January 1986 highlighted the spectacular success of the product and at the end of 1986 it was decided to install lobby ATMs and to ensure that every branch had at least one machine.

Cardcash allowed the Society to provide as much in the way of money transmission services as the building societies regulation allowed. A limited extension of the DCA department to a further 22 branches in Yorkshire and Lancashire took place at the end of 1982 with the help of Barclays who cleared the DCA cheques for the Society. Around this time the Abbey were making noises about setting up some form of cheque account in cooperation with the Co-op bank, but they too were limited by not being able to provide overdrafts or cheque guarantee cards.

Whilst the Society had been proactive in tackling the cost base of its high activity savings accounts there still remained a problem in attracting sufficient funds to satisfy the mortgage demand. This was an industry wide problem and was one that was becoming more acute, as the newly elected Conservative government of 1979 had great plans for expanding home ownership by the sale of council houses.

In response to these concerns the BSA published the Stow Report in 1980. This examined, but dismissed, the idea of raising funds from the wholesale money markets and instead concluded that the traditional retail funds would meet their needs provided the societies started paying more competitive interest rates. Thus the early 1980s were marked by the introduction of many new savings products, all offering a premium on paid up share interest rates but with various restrictions on term of investment or availability of withdrawals. The Halifax's offerings included Term Shares, High Growth bonds, Xtra Interest and Xtra Interest Plus, the various restrictions on these products seemingly changing every month.

Thayre, the traditionalist, had gone on record as saying that he saw that the Society would never have more than 10 per cent of its investments coming from term shares but this turned out to be a forlorn hope as the lion's share of all new investment funds increasingly went into these premium products. The true average cost of investment money was therefore significantly higher than the BSA recommended investors' share rate and as inflation was brought back under some form of control (5 per cent in 1983) the investors were at last starting to get a real rate of return on their money – see appendix 8.

The increasingly competitive position regarding investment rates came to a head in the September of 1983 with the break up of the building society cartel caused by the Abbey National's withdrawal from the interest rates undertaking. Clive Thornton, the Abbey's Chief Executive who was regarded by many as a maverick, had waited until most of his fellow building society CEOs were away attending an international building society conference in Australia before he put in the Abbey's statutory three months' notice of withdrawal to the BSA. In Spalding's absence Macaskill commented:

'The Break-up of the Building Society Cartel' screamed the headlines. In reality it was the last rites that were being performed in public – the patient had died some time previously.

The Stow Report had concluded that because of the relatively low

building society mortgage interest rates, raising funds on the wholesale money markets was a non-starter – however, by 1983 things had changed. Not only had mortgage rates increased relative to money market rates but also the Chancellor of the Exchequer in his 1983 Finance Act allowed building societies to start paying interest gross

Calum Macaskill Deputy Chief General Manager multitasking in 1983

rather than net of tax. Thus in the summer of 1983 it was possible for the Society to raise £100 million from the markets by issuing certificates of deposit (an instrument which was tradable at any time with maturity up to one year). This initial tranche of money was used to bolster the Society's liquid funds thus allowing a larger proportion of new personal savings to flow directly into mortgage lending. This was just the start of a whole new era in which large sums would be raised on the wholesale money markets.

In 1984/1985 the Society raised £100 million on a medium term (five years) basis and the department responsible for the wholesale money markets was renamed Treasurer's Department. Following further relaxations of the rules in the March 1985 Budget, the Society issued £150 million of Floating Rate Notes in the Eurobond market. The Society was certainly not on its own in using the wholesale money markets, the Chief

Registrar (the building societies' regulator) recommending in 1984 a 5 per cent guideline on wholesale funding as a proportion of total funding and then in 1985 saying that he had no problem if wholesale funds exceeded 5 per cent. As time went by it became less easy to distinguish whether these funds raised were for tactical liquidity or just mortgage lending. Interest rate structures were now such that the banks and a new class of centralised lender (eg The Mortgage Corporation) found it particularly attractive to enter the UK's residential mortgage market, creating true competition to the building societies.

By 1986 all differential rates based on mortgage loan size as well as any premium for endowment loans had been dropped. The talk was now all about marketing mortgages, with Hornby stating at the Society's 1985 AGM 'we achieved our aim of bringing mortgage rationing to an end for our members'. From being in a cosy position of selling a product that was in short supply, the movement had had to change to operating in a true market driven economy, this being the result of Margaret Thatcher's economic reforms.

Because of its size and importance to the economy, governments of all colours were always interested in the building society movement. Following the Liverpool Toxteth riots in 1981 Michael Heseltine (Secretary of State for environment) set up a working group of representatives from financial institutes to see how they could help with the problems of the inner city. David Couttie was seconded from the Society and on his return became the Society's housing development controller. Housing development encompassed finance provision for large developments of housing, often multi million pound loans to housing associations, this money usually being provided on a phased basis. This was the start of providing funds for commercial lending and it was hoped that future legislation would allow the power for societies to own and manage land as well as become landlords.

Following the break up of the interest rate undertaking the Halifax board debated the role played by the BSA and concluded that in general it had held back government intervention and probably avoided unwelcome legislation. It was able to provide a collective industry view on issues such as MIRAS (Mortgage Interest Relief At Source), which was introduced in

April 1983. A current major initiative of the BSA was its working group on 'the future constitution and powers of building societies', which held its first meeting in the autumn of 1981. The group was chaired by Spalding of the Halifax and reported its initial thoughts to members in January 1983. The process of introducing any new legislation is, by necessity, a lengthy interactive process – and so it was in this case.

In August 1984 a government green paper was published and eventually the Building Societies Bill became the Building Societies Act on 25 July 1986 when it received the Royal Assent. The bill allowed societies the opportunity to offer new services from the beginning of 1987 once a society had adopted a memorandum setting out the new powers it desired. In the Halifax's case a Special General Meeting was held on 24 November 1986 to adopt a memorandum that included housing subsidiaries, an estate agency service, personal loans and a wider range of insurance services. The Society's money transmission services would be enhanced by the ability to offer overdrafts.

Membership of BACS and EftPos UK, along with their umbrella company APACS, had already been applied for by the Society back in January 1986 after the publication of the Child Report. This report was the banking industry's response to government pressure on restricted practices and it recommended allowing new entrants into the banks' clearing systems.

One provision in the bill was to allow societies to convert from a mutual to a company status (plc), this requiring the approval of two resolutions – a borrowing member's resolution passed by a simple majority and a special resolution approved by not less than 20 per cent of all members qualified to vote. This last requirement was viewed by many societies as unachievable and Spalding himself did not see the plc option as being particularly attractive. The option had been included as a means of raising capital for building societies that had possibly got themselves into trouble by diversification into the new, riskier class 2 (non-residential secured) and class 3 (unsecured) lending.

The branch and agency network was still the major means of providing the Society's services but it was important that these were in the right places. Appendix 11 shows the fastest ever rate of branch opening between 1980 and 1986, with an 80 per cent increase. In spite of this, branches that were not in the correct location were being closed. Similarly, the number of agency outlets was increasing rapidly from around 1,500 in 1980 to over 2,600 by the end of 1986. Eddie Roach, district manager Elland, wrote an article for the 1980 spring edition of *Round the Table*, on the demise of the nearby Stainland agency. The following extracts give a view on how important this type of outlet had been to the Society's business:

> The first recorded appointments were James Watson and George Healey, 1857 – 1867, and they were followed by two family dynasties which lasted for almost a century. ... Certainly the communications which we take for granted did not then exist and the services of a financial institution, and a local one at that, brought into their midst must have provided a very welcome service for these outlying communities.

Not all the Society's agencies were to be found in the premises of accountants, solicitors or estate agents as Roach then comments on the former Outlane agency:

> ... this beguiling agency at Sandwells Butchers Shop might have tempted the weak willed to treat the family to a tasty leg of pork instead of paying the less attractive mortgage subscription.

Even though the Society's agency network was growing certain rationalisation also occurred in outlying areas and Roach explains the reason for this with:

> The wonders of modern transport in the form of a tram service from Halifax provided the first effective means to convey people and their business to Halifax and Elland. As a result of this new link, the individual agencies (at the villages of Outlane, Hollywell Green and Sowood Green) were no longer viable and ultimately the requirements of the area were served by the sole Stainland agency.

The article encapsulated the integral part that so many of the Society's agents played in the local community, this being advantageous to both the agent and the Halifax alike. Ironically in 1985 the number of regions to support this much bigger network was reduced from 12 to eight, casting doubt yet again on the role of the region.

As the new Building Societies Act came into being, a further new initiative to strengthen the Halifax network and protect its source of introduced mortgage business was introduced - the creation of an estate agency service. Derek Taylor, formally General Manager finance, headed up the new venture that aimed to grow initially by acquisition. Other building societies, clearing banks and insurance companies had similar intentions regarding the provision of their own estate agency services, which all added to the premiums that had to be paid to acquire the existing companies.

The board debate on the creation of the service doubted the projected 4 per cent return on capital, especially when it was realised that 75 per cent of the acquisition cost was goodwill. However, it was generally felt that in order to protect their core business the Society could not afford to be without their own estate agency network.

Against the background of an increasing presence on the high street of the Halifax and the other large societies, the Cheltenham and Gloucester (eleventh largest society with assets of approximately 12 per cent of Halifax) were implementing a very different strategy. For their size they had relatively few branches and agents but they did have a savings product that could be opened and serviced through the post - the 'Cheltenham and Gloucester Gold Account'. This account required a minimum balance of £1,000 but provided immediate access and paid a premium of 1 per cent over the normal investor's share rate. The following figures, which were presented to the Halifax board in June 1984, illustrate how successful this strategy was:

Management Expenses (pence per £100 asset)

YEAR	Cheltenham & Gloucester	Halifax
1979	112	100
1980	128	114
1981	116	122
1982	93	125
1983	78	119
10 Year Asset growth	700%	400%

It was never envisaged that the Halifax could become so dependent on a centrally administered postal account but the provision of the Halifax high street network obviously came at a price.

The big social event of 1986 was the running of the 'Halifax Banker', a steam train excursion organised by a team of Head Office enthusiasts.

Organizing committee and driver of 'Halifax Banker' steam excursion 1986

The train went on a return journey from Halifax to Carlisle, being hauled by the City of Wells over the famous Settle to Carlisle line. Tickets for the excursion were sold by the Halifax branch and the train's name reflected that not only was it being run on August bank holiday Saturday, but also that most people in Halifax had always referred to the Halifax Building Society as 'The Bank'.

Earlier in the year, and on a less sanguine note, the board had discussed a paper on arrears, noting that between 1980 and 1986 losses had gone from £38,000 to £2,170,00 and provisions for losses from £170,000 to £2,250,000. This was just the start of things to come!

8

1986 - 1992

The six years following the passing of the 1986 Building Societies Act was a period in which the Society launched more new products and business initiatives than at any other time in its history. This was not just brought about by the powers that were enabled in the Act but also by the competitive marketplace in which it now operated along with possibilities created in the new age of information technology.

The Society's image was also changing with the introduction of the successful Halifax 'X' brand. This was to last for the remainder of the century and took over from the 'biggest building society in the world' advertising logo, which was always under threat from Californian Savings and Loans institutions when the dollar exchange rate was unfavourable.

Calum Macaskill retired in the December of 1986 having started as a graduate in 1947, and for an employee who had been with the Society man and boy, he reached as high a position as anyone since the days of Fred Bentley.

Jim Birrell succeeded him as Operations Director, a position that now took over most of the responsibilities belonging to Nigel Watson, who retired in the February of 1987. Birrell, an accountant, had joined the Society in 1968 at the age of 35 having worked for Price Waterhouse, Empire Stores and latterly as company secretary for a Huddersfield textile company. At the Society he had worked in finance and then as General Manager London (where he was involved through the BSA with issues such as MIRAS and marketable certificates of deposit) and then finally as General Manager marketing. He was well educated, a good conversationalist and was seen as solid and dependable and was now undoubtedly the heir apparent to Spalding.

Birrell eventually took over from Spalding in August 1988 but prior to that the duo had to come to terms with the realities of the new powers enabled in the 1986 Act. Communicating the thoughts and policies of the

Society to the growing number of managers was becoming increasingly difficult via the traditional four national conferences per year. Spalding decided the time was right for one large national conference, which was to be held in Harrogate in April 1987, and to which all of the Society's 800 managers would be invited. The theme of the professionally staged managed conference was the 'X' factor and it was followed by a gala

Jim Birrell Chief Executive in 1988

dinner at Ripley castle where the after dinner speaker was Denis Norden.

In spite of one or two sore heads the following morning, the event was a great success and morale booster. It did, however, give little indication as to what plans the Society had for the future. Of all decisions, the one as to whether the Society should give up its mutual status and become a plc was the most important. Thus, in January 1988, Rothschilds were appointed as advisors on conversion, they being led by Michael Richardson and Simon Linnet. The Society put together a working party for the project comprising Jim Birrell, Richard Wheway (finance), Gren Folwell (finance), Chris Jowett (legal) and David Gilchrist (planning). Many meetings and discussions took place including an away day for the executive at Middlethorpe Hall, York. The conclusions and the recommendations of their work were discussed at the August meeting of the board, which incidentally was the last one that Spalding attended.

Spalding took a back seat on the plc conversion debate as he thought it unfair to influence decisions that he would not personally have to live with. With the possibility of large future fees, Rothschilds not surprisingly recommended conversion, although the view from within their camp was not unanimous. Their arguments were based on less restrictive regulation and the ease with which a plc could raise capital, this being a requirement for future expansion and diversification.

Indications from South Africa and Australia were also that those societies who delayed conversion did not fair as well as those who had taken the plc route at the first opportunity. With the exception of Mike Whitehouse and Richard Wheway, the Society's executive were generally supportive of the Rothschilds' recommendation, although more detailed work on the cost of raising capital as a plc was starting to cast doubts on the conversion option.

The Bank of England had also indicated that were the Society to convert it would not be allowed to diversify quicker than the regulators saw fit. Gren Folwell was particularly supportive because an existing building society was unable to set up a subsidiary bank, something that the Society's treasury division desired in order to assist with wholesale funding.

Jim Birrell led the boardroom debate, Rothschilds not being present and Dick Hornby concluded by asking each individual board member for their view. The board was split, but on balance decided that they could still do all the planned diversification without the need to convert. Hornby himself was fearful that with conversion the focus would shift from the customer to the shareholder. The official board minutes concluded:

> With no clear view prevailing the question became one of gradations of judgement. Need for new capital not as urgent as it had earlier appeared.

The argument was accepted that the issue of conversion would have to be visited again in the future. The outcome caused surprise in certain quarters but was a vindication of the structure of the Halifax and the thorough way in which major strategic decisions were made, even at the expense of possible personal gain.

Interestingly, the Abbey had caught wind of the appointment by the

Halifax of Rothschilds and assumed that the Halifax definitely intended to convert. They had never been as happy as the Halifax to be regulated as a building society and therefore immediately put plans in motion for their own conversion. These were successful with a vote taking place in April 1989 and the Abbey thus became the first UK building society to convert to plc status. David Llewellyn (external consultant) and John Kay (non executive board member) conducted further work on the cost of capital as a plc, concluding that the Society had made the right decision. (Indeed by the time Jon Foulds was in charge at his first board strategy conference the general consensus had swung totally against conversion.)

Two Steps Forward...

With the decision on conversion having been made, one of Birrell's main objectives was to strengthen the Society's capital base. This would be needed to support the new diversified business and was to be achieved by increasing profitability. In June 1989 a new group structure was put in place, the following reporting directly into Birrell:

- ◆ Mike Whitehouse – Operations Director Building Society
- ◆ Derek Taylor – Managing Director Halifax Estate Agencies Ltd
- ◆ Mike Fearnsides – Managing Director Halifax Financial Services
- ◆ Crawford Laughlan – Group Personnel & Services director
- ◆ David Gilchrist – General Manager Corporate Development
- ◆ Richard Wheway – Finance Director.

Whitehouse, Taylor and Laughlan were made full board members with Gren Folwell replacing Richard Wheway on his retirement in October. Richard Wheway had served the Society for 23 years and was remembered for his intellect, charm and high ethical standards, which had been particularly evident throughout the recent plc conversion debate.

The structure was now in place to exploit the powers enabled in the 1986 Act, but developments had started in earnest back at the start of 1987 when two housing subsidiaries, Halifax Homes Ltd and Halifax Urban Renewal Ltd, had been set up to finance land development. In March 1987 a board paper was presented outlining plans for personal unsecured lending, with target loan books of £410 million after one year and

Richard Wheway, retired as Finance Director in 1989

£3,500million after five years. The estate agency business was rapidly expanding with plans put before the board for an eventual network of 630 offices costing £180 million. Indeed, 600 offices were in place by the end of 1988, with all the different companies brought together under a rebranded Halifax Property Services in February 1989. The exercise, which cost £10 million, introduced a common identity using the new green, red and white colours along with the Halifax 'X'.

Money transmission developments were going ahead at a pace, even before the new powers were introduced, with the Society becoming one of the first building societies to be a full member of BACS in June 1987. This reinforced its views on automating transactions wherever possible and allowed it to operate under the same timescales and costs as the banks.

In August 1987 the Society made a formal application to join EftPos UK (electronic funds transfer at point of sale), which was a co-operative venture between the UK banks to launch a debit card system at the point of sale and thus reduce the need for cheques. Such a system had attractions, as it would allow entry into the current account market without going to the trouble and expense of supporting high volume cheque processing.

Although the Society was one of the few members to develop the technical infrastructure for the scheme it never got off the ground due mainly to inter bank squabbling. Barclays subsequently launched a Visa debit card and Midland, Royal Bank of Scotland and NatWest launched the Switch card. In July 1988 a board paper was presented stating that full acceptance of EFTPOS was still some way off and that cheque volumes were still growing at 5 per cent a year. It was therefore proposed that a full-blown current account with cheques should be launched in September 1989 and this was duly delivered under the product name of Maxim.

As usual the systems were to be developed in-house and an in depth investigation into how the UK cheque clearing systems worked was undertaken with visits to see the clearing centres of Barclays, TSB, Midland and Lloyds. It quickly became apparent that there was little documentation as to how the inter bank clearing systems worked but the Society had an advantage in that it had no legacy systems and was starting from scratch.

Barclays, the Society's main bankers, were persuaded to give up their 11 series sort codes ie, 110001 to 119999 thus allowing the Halifax to give every branch its own sort code, the last four digits being the existing branch number eg Sowerby Bridge sort code was 110728 and Halifax was 110001. This was exactly in line with what all the major clearing banks did and, coupled together with an eight digit account number, gave ample room for any future expansion.

Barclays were to continue collecting all of the Society's cheques, as there was no administrative or cost advantage in setting up a Halifax clearing centre. This decision was further strengthened by the talk of future 'truncation', a process which would mean that only the relevant data from the cheque would be sent to the issuing bank rather than the paper cheque itself. The major difference in the Society's cheque processing when compared with the banks was that it would clear and post all its cheques centrally rather than delivering them to individual branches for them to do the work manually.

Full enquiry and data input facilities for the current accounts were made available to all the branches and Head Office through the terminal network, something which could not have been provided by a 'bought in' or outsourced solution. Even though the Society was going into competition with the clearing banks, there was still a feeling of joining a gentleman's club where respect and co-operation were the order of the day – these two qualities being essential for the successful running of the UK clearing systems.

Cardcash was still growing in popularity, with the Society having over 1,000 ATMs installed by the end of 1988. Other major competitors were now starting to catch up, especially by being a member of one of the shared networks. With the imminent launch of the current account it was felt that the time was now right to help form a truly national ATM network, or risk left being isolated. The existing sharing arrangements were:

◆ Four Banks – Barclays, Lloyds, Royal Bank of Scotland and Bank of Scotland
◆ Midland, Natwest and TSB
◆ LINK – Abbey, Nationwide, Co-op etc
◆ Matrix – Leeds plus other smaller building societies.

The first two bank networks were not branded or well publicised, in contrast to LINK and Matrix who were to merge in the spring of 1989 under the LINK brand. By joining the enhanced LINK network of 2,200 ATMs in July 1989, the Halifax's 1,200 ATMs helped form a credible competitor to the banks. For each ATM withdrawal performed for another bank or building society the ATM owner in the LINK network received a payment from the card issuer of around 35 pence. In order to encourage customers to use Halifax ATMs wherever possible, the Society initially introduced a fee of 50 pence if a customer used a non Halifax ATM. It was therefore not surprising that from the outset of joining LINK the Halifax was a net acquirer of transactions, which generated a healthy income of several million pounds per annum.

In October 1990 the Halifax offered its Maxim customers Switch debit cards, thus becoming the first new organisation to join the Switch scheme after the founding three banks. These electronic Switch transactions were considerably cheaper than the equivalent cheque transaction, especially as the Society actually received 4.75p for every transaction processed. Switch fraud was also much less than that experienced by Visa, mainly because a larger proportion of the transactions was authorised online. It proved to be extremely successful at reducing the use of cheques in retail outlets and by August 1991 Maxim customers had performed over 1 million Switch transactions.

The final piece in the money transmission jigsaw was the need to provide a credit card. An interesting and different approach was taken with the provision of the Halifax Visa card in that it was initially set up as a joint venture with the Bank of Scotland, who would administer the product at their Dunfermline credit card centre. The venture, which was set up in 1988, was budgeted to run at a loss initially because of the heavy costs of growing a customer base.

The desire to strengthen the Society's capital base translated into efforts to reduce the cost/income ratio of the core business. Whitehouse took on board the challenge and ramped up many of the money transmission fees such as those charged for using a LINK ATM, failed standing orders and direct debits along with an annual £10 fee for the Society's Visa card.

Where he really was ahead of his time was with his treatment of uneconomic accounts – low balance, high activity passbook accounts. In 1989 a minimum opening balance of £25 was instigated for passbook accounts, this being increased to £50 in 1991 and the payment of no interest should the balance drop below £50. Whilst the board expressed reservations regarding the Society's image with the small investor, Whitehouse argued that the Cardcash and Maxim non-passbook accounts were the correct products for these customers. The initiative had the desired effect but was later dropped under Mike Blackburn with the adoption of the Leeds passbook accounts that had optional plastic cards. The move away from the counter towards using ATMs was to come back with a vengeance during the early part of the next century when Andy Hornby was in charge.

Selling life assurance products continued much as before with the Halifax remaining an independent intermediary. However, in the March of 1989 this decision was reversed and the Society became a tied agent of Standard Life, with a small independent subsidiary (later to be called Halifax Independent Financial Advisors Ltd - HIFAL) still selling other life company products should the customer want them.

In the final quarter of 1990 Global Advantage, a PEP and unit trust, was launched which was a joint venture between the Halifax and Standard Life. By the end of the decade there was much internal talk and speculation about the possibility of a new financial services company being formed from Halifax, Standard Life and Bank of Scotland. Halifax had a major joint venture with the two Scottish companies and Standard life was a large shareholder in the bank. No merger took place, not this time, and as with many joint ventures different objectives meant that the partnerships only lasted for a few years. Nevertheless the Halifax had gained significant experience of two new areas of operation when they took 100 per cent control of the Halifax Visa card in 1995 and set up their own life company in the same year.

At one time Europe was seen as a great opportunity for growth, but it was not easy to see what expertise or knowledge was transferable to any continental operation. If the Society had really been serious it would have bought an existing European operation, but maybe it felt that it could risk enough capital on ventures within the UK. In the early 1990s there were several projects initiated to look into the purchase of such a European operation, these projects being clothed in secrecy and given strange names such as 'Marmalade', but none came to fruition. Finally a small-scale operation was set up in Spain, opening an office in Madrid in July 1994.

With the business potential created by the new products and cross selling opportunities it was not surprising that a fundamental review of the branch network was undertaken. This review led to an expansion in the total amount of branch space used for selling to customers but also resulted in a modest reduction in the absolute number of branches from 1990 onwards – see appendix 11.

In 1987 the 'Branch 2000' project started with the aim of providing a better selling environment by the use of friendly open plan counselling areas that were constructed to ensure privacy. Counters were also redesigned to have a less hostile interface with the customers by removing the permanent bandit screens, and instead use quick rise bandit screens or pneumatic air tube systems for the transmission of cash.

Common branding (using the Halifax 'X') and signage was used wherever possible to create a universal image of the Society. At the end of 1988 over 100 branches had been converted, but increased use of branch office space for the customer often meant more cramped accommodation for the back office administrative staff. A solution to this problem was found by removing the office administration from the branch to regional

London Kensington branch July 1988. The first branch to be converted to "Branch 2000" format, incorporating the Halifax X logo.

service centres. These centres varied in size but would typically support between 12 and 20 branches, the Sheffield service centre being the first to be put in place. There were many problems to overcome, not least being that staff had to choose whether they wanted to work in the branch selling environment or move to work on administration in the service centre.

A group of personnel from BIS (Business Information Systems – the Society's IT division) visited the Sheffield service centre in January 1989, shortly after it had been set up. What shocked them as they walked round was the sight of a large administrative office using equipment that had been designed for, and transferred from, much smaller branch offices – ie, small numeric only keyboards, 40 character single line displays and slow 132 characters per second passbook printers. What they really required was the same equipment as used by Head Office administration departments – full alphanumeric keyboards with VDUs and laser printers.

Some of the service centre problems could be solved by spending money and providing more appropriate equipment, others would take considerably longer as fundamental software changes were required to the Society's basic accounting systems. Chief of these was the concept that a branch could only enter many types of data for its own accounts, every account being allocated to just one specific branch. For the service centres, which were now administering several branches, this constraint caused severe logistical problems. Following the visit, major software changes were set in motion that would allow any of the Society's terminals to update accounts for any branch. This marked the end of an era when customers and staff alike knew who was responsible for the integrity of an account ie, the controlling branch.

Other areas such as telephone systems needed much more serious consideration but the ambitious plans for the network dictated a roll out of a further 12 service centres during the rest of the year.

There was a feeling that these changes were happening so fast that the sacrosanct image of administrative excellence, on which the Halifax so prided itself, was in real danger of being lost forever. Later on in 1989 Whitehouse was so worried that he personally took control, making network strategy the responsibility of the whole building society team and not just the domain of the field operations division. Customer service again became the number one priority.

BIS, the IT division, was commissioned to provide new PC based quotation systems that could be used in the new branch selling environment for the increasingly complex mortgage and new Standard Life products. Initially bought-in software packages were used but they proved to be inflexible and slow to develop. In response to these problems a set of development tools and reusable software routines were developed for the PC platform by the Society's own IT staff. This system was initially called X-SELL reflecting the Halifax 'X' and its cross selling objective. However, the 'S' changed to 'C' for Customer and the name XCEL was born. XCEL was an immediate hit, with users soon requesting further functionality. In the first five years of the XCEL system, a suite of 18 applications was developed, all specifically supporting Halifax products and associated administration.

XCEL eventually replaced the old Philips PTS 6000 system, which had provided sterling service for over 15 years. Having the capability to change software on both the PC and mainframe platforms, BIS were able to produce some very powerful workflow systems called XTRAS, the first ones being developed for arrears control. Not everything, however, was plain sailing with the XCEL sales support systems. In June 1991 a group of BIS personnel visited Liverpool to see how one of the newly developed XCEL HFSL (Halifax Financial Services Ltd) systems was working. Contrary to design objectives, it soon became apparent that the XCEL system was not being used at all when the sales staff were interviewing the prospective customer. All the regularity checks so painstakingly developed to ensure the sales process was compliant, were seen as being obstructive to the clinching of a sale! Commission based sales staff obviously had totally different objectives from Head Office compliance officers.

... And one step back

Exciting times they were and all the new initiatives were tackled with great enthusiasm, but surprisingly the first area to cause concern was the core mortgage business. During the 1970s high house price inflation was followed by periods where price rises were much lower than the general rate of inflation, but prices never decreased in absolute terms.

The situation that occurred in the early 1990s was totally different. Things started to go wrong in April 1988 when Nigel Lawson set 1 August 1988 as the date when it would no longer be possible for more than one person to claim MIRAS tax relief on a single property. This created a boom in demand for mortgages ahead of the deadline thus adding to the effect on house prices of strong earnings growth and falling

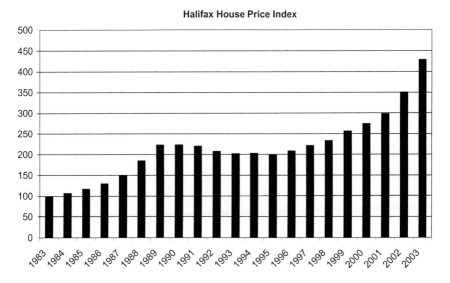

Halifax House Price Index

unemployment. To correct an overheated economy, interest rates rose to such an extent that the Society was charging a mortgage rate of 13.5 per cent by the end of its financial year (31 January 1989). UK house prices peaked in the summer of 1989 and did not recover their value until March 1998.

The situation experienced during the later part of 1989 and the early 1990s has no modern day equivalent, with property values falling in a period when mortgage rates were high. The expression 'negative equity' was increasingly being used to describe the situation where the mortgage was greater than the value of the property. Customers walked into Halifax branches in order to throw in their house keys, in the mistaken belief that this action discharged them of their mortgage responsibilities. Not surprisingly the arrears situation worsened dramatically with the number of properties in possession doubling during 1991 to over 10,000. Insurance companies who had provided the mortgage guarantee cover (insurance for any loss on loans over 75 per cent of the property valuation) were alarmed at the number of claims and their magnitude – average loss of £18,000 for each possession case. Provisions for losses on residential property went up 50 fold between 1989 and 1994.

This collapse in house prices was not unique to the Halifax, but the Society was at the forefront of dealing with the problem by actively managing the arrears and possessions early on and adopting a conservative

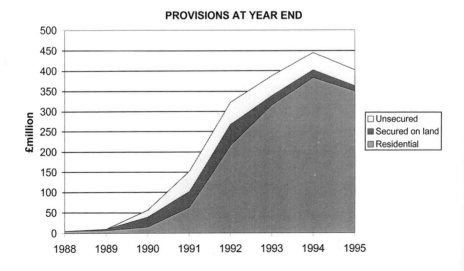

PROVISIONS AT YEAR END

approach to all new lending with regard to income multiples and loan/value ratio. The Society adopted a sympathetic attitude towards customers who were having difficulty with their mortgage repayments - the term that started to be used was 'forbearance'. A mortgage rescue scheme was launched whereby a borrower could become a tenant in the property they previously owned, but the scheme had few takers. In spite of the tightening of controls the Society managed to maintain its asset based share of any new lending.

The high interest rates that were being used to control the economy were also having an effect on other areas of the Society's business. In July 1989 Kentish Homes Ltd collapsed and the Society appointed a receiver to take control of the Burrells Wharf Development for which it had provided funding. Further development companies went into receivership, notable amongst these being Declan Kelly in February 1990 to which the Society had lent £39 million.

A deteriorating property market exposed the naivety with which the Society had entered the commercial lending market. In May 1990 two commercial lending bankers from the Bank of Scotland were seconded to the Society in order to provide some much needed expertise. All new lending was suspended except to registered housing associations. The management of the existing portfolio was centralised in Halifax under Fraser Mackay, one of the Scottish bankers on secondment, and the diversification into financing speculative property development came to an abrupt end.

The downturn in the property market also had its effect on Halifax Property Services (HPS). The ownership of an estate agency was seen as a defensive measure, put in place to protect the Society's mortgage business. Having spent over £300 million putting the network together the board wanted to see a reasonable return on its capital investment. At their September 1989 meeting they were far from happy to hear that HPS was heading for a £30 million loss for the year. They thought this unacceptable and set a target of reducing it to at least £20 million. In the event the business came in with a loss of £27 million, followed by losses of £18.3 million, £6.6 million and £14.8 million in the following three years.

Just as soon as the rebranded network was completed, rationalisation and closure of offices started to take place. It would have been difficult to predict the severity and duration of the downturn in the housing market. However, what is clear is that the Halifax, along with other mortgage providers, bought into estate agents at the top of the market at far too high a price. Estate agency is very much a business based on local knowledge and expertise and it was not altogether obvious what advantages a large national network such as HPS brought to the customer.

Unsecured personal loans was another product which was not living up to expectations. It had been assumed that they could be sold and administered through the branches in much the same way as a mortgage. Initially they were only available to customers with an existing mortgage and little bad debt was experienced. As the rules were relaxed and the product was sold to other than existing borrowers the bad underwriting and poor arrears control were exposed. It had been assumed that, just like a mortgage, there was no need for serious action until the third missed payment had been experienced, and then it would be in the form of an arrears letter. One branch manager on being told that one of his unsecured loans was beyond any hope commented that he would just have to sell another one to make up for the loss. Such was the lack of understanding of this product in an organisation that had always had the security of a property to back up any loan.

The losses being experienced were such as to cause the Society to think of closing down the product. In fact the selling of the product was suspended in mid 1990 in certain areas of north London where fraud was particularly prevalent. In order to improve the arrears situation personal loan debt recovery was centralised in Halifax and a new debt recovery system was implemented which provided terminal enquiry and chase procedures coupled into an integrated power dialling telephony system – a first for the Halifax. The concept of telephoning customers in arrears after six o'clock in the evenings or at weekends was alien to the more conservative staff, but this is what the new world of unsecured lending necessitated. Through hard work and concentrating on quality, the product was turned round and made profitable, but the size of the loan book after five years was only 10 per cent of that which was forecast in the original paper to the board in 1987.

Steady As She Goes

Against the background of the new Building Societies Act, new products and administrative changes, the normal business was also growing and changing. There was much concern at the time about the IRA bombing campaign and their attack on the NatWest Tower in the city of London. In 1986, and partly as a response to this threat, a new data centre and warehouse at Copley was proposed, which was to be built on a secure green field site with a perimeter fence. In 1988 the deed store in the basement of the Head Office was significantly re-engineered and expanded so as to accommodate a new maximum capacity of two and a half million deeds, even though the number of borrowers was then just over one and a half million.

Banks were allowed to pay a composite rate of tax (CRT) on investment interest in 1986, so bringing them into line and giving them the same advantage as building societies. The advantage of CRT had become significantly less over the years as the composite rate as a percentage of standard rate tax went up from 55 per cent in 1953 to 85 per cent in 1986.

Left to right: Andrew Dickson, Divisional Manager, Richard Barrow, General Manager, Dick Hornby, Chairman and Jim Birrell Chief Executive look on as HRH Prince Charles signs the visitors' book on his visit to the Copley data center on 24th October 1989.

Eventually on 6 April 1991 CRT was abolished with the Society allowing customers to opt for an interest payment being made on 5 April so as to take full advantage of this last occurrence of reduced taxation.

Investors were now charged a flat rate of 20 per cent on their interest with higher rate taxpayers having to declare interest payments on their tax returns. Investors who did not use all of their personal tax allowance (eg most children) could now fill out an R85 form thus allowing them to have their interest paid gross of tax. In order to control the customer declaration on these R85 forms, a centralised microfilming system was developed which cross-referenced the declaration to the computer records. Whilst this is perhaps a trivial example, it illustrates a pronounced trend in centralising ever more administration. Indeed it became a moot point as to how many staff employed at the 'Halifax Head Office' were indeed Head Office staff as opposed to general account administration staff. These staff could have been sited anywhere in the country but it was much easier to control all the operations from the one town, albeit split over several sites within Halifax.

Without a doubt the 1986 Building Societies Act was a major turning point in the history of the Society. John Spalding's work on behalf of the building society industry was officially recognised in March 1988 when he was invested as a Commander of the Order of the British Empire. In the meantime Birrell had to deal with some of the most turbulent years experienced by any Chief Executive of the Halifax.

9

20 OCTOBER 1992

They say that lightning never strikes the same place twice, but there are some similarities between the Fred Bentley affair and the events that culminated on the evening of 20 October 1992.

At the end of July 1990 Dick Hornby retired after being Chairman since 1983. Jim Birrell, his Chief Executive, obviously had a good rapport with him as is shown in his comments at his retirement:

> Dick Hornby is a man of great wisdom, humanity and sensitivity … a man who clearly personifies the best qualities of the Society.

Jon Foulds, another Lancastrian, succeeded Dick Hornby as Chairman. In spite of similarity of their birthplace they were essentially very different people. Foulds had been Chief Executive and Deputy Chairman of the venture capitalist 3i Group, his other business interests including Mercury Asset Management and Eurotunnel. His background and experience came from the city and he was not as naturally at ease with what he regarded as a somewhat steady, parochial, mutual organisation. That said he was certainly impressed by the size of the organisation and its balance sheet and he had been convinced by the arguments put forth in favour of remaining mutual. Birrell stated that he respected both of the Chairmen he worked with, recognising that they had different qualities. He did however appear to be much more at ease with Hornby than Foulds.

Foulds wanted to be more involved in the day-to-day running of the organisation. Prior to his chairmanship, the executive held several strategic away day conferences at Middlethorpe Hall, York, but no non-executive directors were present. The last one in this

Jon Foulds, Chairman 1990 – 1999

format was in January 1990 where a review took place of all the developments that had occurred since the 1986 Act. Its conclusion was that the executive was lukewarm on a merger, but that one was within the realms of possibility. However, it was agreed that the Standard Life/ Bank of Scotland/ Halifax relationship should be developed further.

By the time of the January 1991 conference Foulds had significant input - its venue was moved to New Hall, Sutton Coldfield and the attendees now included all of the board. Indeed the event was called the 'Directors Strategy Conference' with David Gilchrist co-ordinating the work on preparing the discussion papers. Birrell accepted Foulds' greater involvement in certain operational areas such as commercial lending, where indeed the Society was short of expertise. Foulds, for his part, did not want to manage any of the operations but he was interested in ensuring that the board and executive were of the right calibre, once suggesting that it might be a good idea to bring in some MBAs to be Regional General Managers. He established a London Corporate Office at Cornhill in the city, which he used as his London base and also for corporate entertaining. One of his and the board's most important tasks was to appoint a successor to Birrell who was due to retire in1993 at the age of 60.

The tradition at the Society had been to appoint its next Chief Executive from within the organisation, albeit most of them had had a career elsewhere prior to joining the Halifax. Unlike when Birrell had been appointed Chief Executive there was no consensus of opinion amongst the executive as to who should take over the top job. The current executive directors were Crawford Laughlan (also retiring 1993), Gren Folwell, Derek Taylor and Mike Whitehouse. Folwell and Taylor were both accountants with experience outside the Halifax, but whatever ambitions Taylor might have had were not helped by his move to be Managing Director of HEAL (Halifax Estate Agency Ltd). Folwell no doubt regarded himself as a candidate for the job in spite of having little knowledge or experience of the operational side of the business.

Whitehouse, by contrast, knew the core building society business inside out. Like many of the Society's employees he had joined on leaving school at the age of 16 and had been a member of the computer department since its inception. The early years of computerisation allowed those working in the department to fully understand and document, for the first time, all aspects of the Society's administration. This knowledge base, along with his determination and eye for detail, allowed him to progress through the management ranks, working initially under David Gilchrist and Mike Fearnsides, but all the time being seen as the protégé of Calum Macaskill. In 1989 he was reluctantly persuaded to take over Birrell's key Operations Director role, thus leaving the power base of the computer department (Business Information Systems). Shortly after taking on this new role he attended Harvard Business School for three months, as had become the norm for the Society's top executives. On his return he bumped into Sue Boyd, one of the Society's solicitors, who asked him how he had got on at Harvard. His reply in many ways typified the man when he said:

> I learnt that I had been doing it right all along.

Whitehouse firmly believed in delivering quality products and systems and his many initiatives designed to address the problems of profitability, loss provisions and arrears of the late 1980s early 1990s were most opportune. In response to the branches many varied and sometimes lax interpretation of Head Office guidelines Whitehouse introduced a series of key controls, covering everything from mortgage loan application to ATM operation procedures. Although this strict command and control style of management was not universally

Mike Whitehouse, Building Society Operations Director 1989 – 1992

popular, it did have the desired effect of turning the business round.

Foulds was impressed by these actions to improve the Society's profitability and still maintain its asset-based share of new business. The dual objectives of profitability and growth, which Foulds always supported, were the subject of frequent debate and were often seen as mutually exclusive. Whitehouse, similar to Macaskill, felt that the Society was large enough to go for growth rather than short-term profitability.

Whitehouse was certainly extremely knowledgeable and committed to the Society, as was apparent to his many visitors at Head Office, who would be given a whistle stop tour of all the departments and invariably had a demonstration of all the latest IT systems. These visitors received more information from Whitehouse in two hours than they would normally get from other people in two weeks, with visitors from abroad often enquiring whether it would be possible to purchase the Society's impressive IT system.

Birrell and others accepted that Whitehouse was exceptional operationally, but felt that he was lacking in diplomacy, especially about other people's shortcomings. Undoubtedly Foulds held this view, but before he made any final decision on succession he asked a newcomer to the board, Nigel Colne of Marks & Spencer, to provide him with feedback following a day he spent with Whitehouse and his team. This took place on 13 October 1992 and was organised by Whitehouse to give Colne a better understanding of the retail business, it concluding with dinner at Holdsworth House in the evening. All appeared to go well with the day's visit but Colne reported back to Foulds, confirming the doubts about Whitehouse's suitability for the Chief Executive's job.

The October board meeting was on Wednesday 21, and on the previous Tuesday evening I gave a presentation to the board on the Society's IT strategy. The request for this presentation was brought about by lobbying from IT consultancy companies who were being thwarted in their attempts to do business with the Society. Of particular concern to these companies was the Society's use of the IBM Assembler programming language, this in their mind being old fashioned and therefore casting doubt on the judgment of the BIS management. Indeed other people within the organisation, having no knowledge of the difference between Assembler and any other computer language, reiterated these concerns from time to time. Therefore Foulds wanted his board to affirm, in their own minds, that the current strategy was indeed sensible.

The presentation summarised the alternative current possibilities for developing systems as being the use of packages or some form of high-level language. These approaches all had a down side for an organisation the size of the Halifax, namely in terms of efficiency, flexibility and integration with existing systems. In contrast the Society's use of

Assembler, with many internally developed aids, tools and a library of several thousand commonly used routines, had provided a platform that was extremely efficient and flexible and also dramatically reduced the time taken to develop systems.

Marketing executive Peter Wood using a Keyfax terminal

The flexibility of using Assembler had allowed the Society to deliver a large degree of integration between all its systems. This integration had many benefits including the development of a sophisticated customer information file (CIF) whereby a total customer relationship was made available to sales people and the direct marketing division. Another benefit was the provision of an extremely comprehensive management information system that was available to all branches and Head Office departments and given the internal name of 'Keyfax'. The delivery of this system was through a cheap dial up 'Viewdata' terminal and Keyfax was in many ways ahead of its time and could be seen as a forerunner to today's Internet and Intranet systems.

The conclusion to the evening's presentation was that a major strength of the Society was the experience and business understanding of its IT staff. Its success should be judged on what it delivered rather than on what programming language it used. The presentation appeared to be successful in addressing the old 'bogey' of the Society's use of IBM Assembler language, but the issue was never to go away as others from time to time would again raise the question, often in order to further their own causes.

Whitehouse was on a high after the presentation, which had given support to many of his long held beliefs on how IT should be used within the organisation, the Halifax's IT systems being in his own mind second to none. The board, Foulds and especially Birrell, however, had other things on their mind as the rest of us went for dinner in the director's dining room. After the first course people were asking where Birrell and Whitehouse were and why hadn't they come into dinner. The answer was simple – whilst the rumour was that Whitehouse was to be the next Chief Executive, Birrell was actually explaining to him that his career with the Halifax was at an end. He saw him to the lift on fourth floor, Whitehouse leaving the building, which he would not enter again until 2003 when he was invited back to celebrate the Halifax's 150th year. Many of us ended up the evening in Derek Taylor's conservatory in Skircoat Green, discussing the evening's momentous event over a beer. Although Whitehouse's departure was not totally unexpected, the way in which it was carried out certainly was, with a feeling that what was happening was more akin to events that occurred in a Harvard Business School case study.

The next morning Foulds addressed the executive prior to the board meeting. For once the confident and ice cool image that the Chairman invariably exuded was not evident as he showed signs of nervousness and explained his thoughts that 'Whitehouse was a jewel but nevertheless a flawed jewel'. Even though many of the executives could understand the personality conflict, there was no doubt an element of unease regarding the abrupt manner of Whitehouse's departure. However, what was really being played out was a struggle for power between the Chairman and the executive and Foulds had long since detected a split amongst them regarding their views on Whitehouse as a succession candidate for the top job.

Whitehouse had stated all along to both Birrell and Foulds that he was not interested in being Chief Executive - but he may have been open to persuasion. Foulds, however, never really tried to encourage him to take on the job and had come to the conclusion that a Chief Executive recruited from outside the Society would find it extremely difficult to work with and manage Whitehouse. As well as wanting a new Chief Executive, Foulds also needed a new General Manager Personnel and his aim was to recruit both from outside the organisation. By the following summer Mike

Blackburn and John Lee had been appointed to these two strategic roles. Jim Birrell retired in August 1993 having being made a Knight Bachelor, an honour bestowed to reflect his leadership of the Halifax, which had shown a responsible attitude to borrowers in difficult times. Indeed, Birrell had successfully led the Society through one of its most challenging periods since its centenary in 1953.

Mike Blackburn's previous position was as Chief Executive of the Leeds Permanent, the country's fifth largest building society. His career encompassed a period as Chief Executive of the Joint Credit Card Company (Access) and before that he had worked for Lloyds bank. John Lee came from a career with ICI where he ended up as International Personnel Manager. In November 1993, after a clause in his termination contract preventing him from working for a competitor had expired, Whitehouse moved down south to take up a position as Operations Director at NatWest bank. A further clause in the contract prevented him from taking the issue of his termination of employment to the Society's members – perhaps indicating fear of a repeat of the Fred Bentley affair!

Whitehouse's dismissal marked the end of an era where 'administration was king' and customer service was all important. The baton for the cause had previously been held by the likes of Alexander Thompson and Calum Macaskill, but never again were people who truly understood the administration of the business to be seen at board level. Every dog has its day, and the top dogs in the future were to come from other backgrounds such as finance and marketing.

A final anecdote to these events regards a visit that took place to see the Head Office nurse, Sister Hagan. In the reception area were piles of leaflets regarding 'stress in the workplace'. On enquiring as to whether there were many cases of employees suffering from stress, she answered in the affirmative saying that there had been a marked increase since Mike Whitehouse's departure. 'Surely you mean a decrease' said the visitor knowing the demands Whitehouse could put his staff under. 'No' said Sister Hagan, 'there has been a marked increase, caused by much greater uncertainty about the future'.

10

1993 - 1997

Mike Blackburn was strong on image, this being helped by his easily recognised smiling face and his interest in the theatre. He settled into his new job by taking stock of the situation – talking to members of staff and visiting branches.

The sheer scale and diversity of the Halifax's operation when compared with the Leeds could not be ignored. Annual profits of £680 million (in spite of an estate agency loss of £18.3 million and overall provisions for losses of £374 million) were reported in March 1993, second only to Lloyds bank, with Barclays bank reporting a loss for the first time ever. Under difficult trading conditions the Halifax's market share of net mortgage lending had been 24.7 per cent, way above its asset based share of existing mortgages.

This success was no doubt a challenge to Blackburn who somehow had to take the business onto even bigger and better things. Given the hiatus created by Whitehouse's departure, the Society's senior management were keen to know what major changes Blackburn had in mind for the organisation. For his part Blackburn was not to be rushed, giving little away but encouraging more self-examination by the use of extensive

City reception for Sir James Birrel's retirement 7th July 1993.
Left to right: Stephen Cockroft, Chris Jowett, David Gilchrist, Mike Ellis, Derek Taylor, Mike Blackburn, Sir James Birrell, Gren Folwell, Mike Fearnsides, Dick Spelman, Geoff Jackson, Richard Barrow and John Lee.

market research, mystery shopper programmes and a revamped staff suggestion scheme. He felt that to a certain extent the Society was too smug about its success and that it should benchmark itself, not just with other financial organisations, but also the likes of BT, IBM and Marks & Spencer. Both he and John Lee disliked the 'key control' culture that was still in existence, much preferring to loosen the controls on the front line staff so that they could run the business unhindered by Head Office dictates.

In early 1994 he took the executive off for the day to Holdsworth House, a hotel on the outskirts of Halifax, to discuss the Society's mission statement. Two things remain in my mind regarding the day, the first being an incident where a bird flew out of the fireplace of the room in which we were taking morning coffee. Building Society executives must have a phobia of such birds as the room was cleared in two seconds flat, leaving just David Gilchrist, Geoff Jackson and myself to coax the bird out of one of the windows. The second and more important thing was how pleased Blackburn was regarding the outcome of the day's discussions, which was the new mission statement, to be:

The biggest and best personal finance business in the UK.

In truth it was little different to its predecessor, which was admittedly wordier and mentioned being a 'leading retail financial services group' rather than the 'biggest and best'. Interestingly this new mission statement only lasted for two years before it reverted back to being 'a leading provider of personal financial services'.

Over the next few months much effort and planning was put into how this new mission statement would be 'cascaded' down to all the Society's employees. A national conference was organised, to take place at the ICC Birmingham in the November of 1994, where the new mission statement was to be the principal theme. To those involved in the complexities of running the organisation the emphasis on the new mission statement seemed a little over the top. However, to Blackburn the new mission statement supported the playing of an extremely important trump card. The changing of the adjective 'leading' to 'biggest' was to help him in his yet to be announced desire to merge with his old society the Leeds Permanent.

In the 12 month period since he had left them, the Leeds had been in a state of shock, their board being unable to appoint a successor. The two internal candidates, Roger Boyes and John Miller, either did not want the job or were not seen as suitable. The board had then spent precious time wooing David O'Brien of the National & Provincial to merge with them and become their new chief executive. Not surprisingly these talks had broken down as they found out, what most other people in the building society world already knew, that O'Brien was a maverick with an unusual management style.

In the spring of 1994 Blackburn bumped into Miller at one of the corporate sponsored sporting events they were both attending, and subsequent discussions that day led to a whole series of secret meetings between Blackburn, Miller and Boyes aimed at merging the two societies. Given their not altogether happy experience of the previous year, Miller, Boyes and the rest of the Leeds board needed little convincing of the soundness of such a merger that would reunite them with their lost and much admired leader.

The benefits of the merger were not quite as obvious to the Halifax directors, but having signed up to the new mission statement it was difficult to argue against it. The possibilities of mergers had been discussed in the past but it had always been felt that the benefits were outweighed by the problems and work involved in merging the administration and cultures of two separate organisations. Certainly a merger or takeover of a small society was never seen as worthwhile. Even merging with a society the size of the Leeds, which was just under a third the size of the Halifax, hardly created a new organisation operating in a different league. Nevertheless a merger had always been attractive to Folwell, Ellis (Mike Ellis, General Manager Treasury and European Operations) and Foulds with their contacts in the city and with Whitehouse gone there was no champion for the opposition.

One other major consideration was the requirement to have firm plans in place to convert the newly merged organisation to plc status. This was a prerequisite of the Leeds board and was needed to guarantee the support of the Leeds members for the merger. Without any financial inducement members may as well wait for a potential takeover and subsequent payout by one of the banks, along the lines of the recent acquisition of the Cheltenham & Gloucester by Lloyds bank. This financial windfall would also assist in getting Halifax members to vote for the merger and it did not require too much thought to realise that merger and conversion must go hand in hand. Ignoring any benefits brought about by a merger, the arguments for conversion had changed little since the last time they were debated by the board in 1988. However, what had changed was the composition of the board with the departure of Wheway, Whitehouse and Hornby the balance of opinion had now shifted towards the need for conversion.

The September board meeting allowed the executive non-directors to listen to the thoughts of the board on the merger and to give any input they thought fit. I was the only person who was wary, especially of the administrative complications, quoting that the recent merger between the Nationwide and the Anglia had internally been tortuous and had meant them taking their eye off the ball for the last five years.

The Halifax board, however, was on a high, had already decided that the merger made excellent sense and were not to be swayed by any problems of an operational nature. Meetings continued in secret and by the time of the national conference at the ICC on 1 November 1994 all members of the executive committee were made aware of the discussions but were sworn to secrecy. The conference was very upbeat about the Society going forward to be the 'biggest and the best' with few of the participants having any inkling of the prospective merger. The national press were, however, better informed and by 25 November the two societies had no option but to make an official announcement and stop any possible speculative investments designed to take advantage of conversion to plc status.

In one fell swoop Blackburn had made the impact he had so desired and put an end to the months of waiting. He was also subtly encouraging other initiatives designed to challenge the Halifax culture of Head Office control and command. Encouragement was given to people to challenge practices and procedures for which they were not directly responsible.

One such initiative was the 'Working Practices Review of the house-moving process' which was based in the West Kent service centre under the leadership of Margaret Walkinshaw. What started off as an independent project within the branch network, in months had turned into one that produced a long shopping list of changes required from Head Office divisions, especially technology. Some of the ideas, such as workflow management, were sound but needed significant resources to integrate them properly with the existing IT systems. When it became apparent that these resources were not available, consultants, including McKinsey, were brought in to try and fill the gap. Walkinshaw took centre stage at the Society's November conference announcing that the pilot 'hassle free service for people moving house' was already a success and would be rolled out to other regions of the Society's network. It is debatable what the project really delivered, but the initiative certainly challenged the existing, clearly defined, management structure of the Society. This exercise in devolving power was a watershed after which it became increasingly more difficult to know where specific responsibilities lay.

Against the background of a new Chief Executive and a significant merger in the offing it is easy to forget that the traditional business was not standing still. The major initiative of the period was the launch of Halifax Life in the January of 1995. A board decision had been made back in August 1993 to terminate the commission based, tied relationship with Standard life and provide the Society's own Halifax Life products.

In March 1994 James Crosby joined the Society to become Managing Director of Halifax Life and take over total responsibility for HFSL (Halifax Financial Services Ltd) from Mike Fearnsides when he retired in June 1994. Crosby had previously been a General Manager with Scottish Amicable Life Assurance Society and a non-executive director with J Rothschild Assurance Holdings. Not only did he bring with him a lot of relevant experience, but he was also seen as being well educated, well connected, intelligent and personable. He quickly nailed his colours to the 'quality mast' telling everyone that Halifax Life must be for the long term, building on the trust that the public had with the Halifax brand. There was already evidence of HFSL sales personnel cutting corners by fabricating interview records in order to sell more products and earn more commission. He set about correcting these problems by introducing further training and tighter management of the sales force. His emphasis on quality was undoubtedly correct, as compliance became an even bigger issue in the years to follow.

Tight timescales and lack of experience dictated that the Society could not develop its own administrative procedures for Halifax Life products, although new front-end selling systems were developed on the XCEL platform. Data was collected centrally in Halifax and then

James Crosby Chief Executive 1999

transmitted to General Accident and S G Warburg for processing. The purchase of Clerical Medical in 1996, whose particular strength was in the Independent Financial Advisor sector, complemented Halifax Life's branch based sales, diversifying the Society further into life assurance.

The general insurance business was also changing with the launch of Halifax Motor Insurance at the end of 1996 and the bringing of household policy and claims processing in-house during the same year. The latter initiative was an interesting reversal of the general move to outsource processing wherever possible, but here it gave more control and understanding of the total product that could then be reflected in future pricing and marketing strategies. This approach was very much in line with traditional Halifax strategies of being in control of all aspects of the support and administration of a product.

In February 1995 Business TV was launched to help Head Office communicate with the branch network and in March of the same year Halifax Direct was launched, offering a direct telephone service for customers.

However, the project that was of most concern and took up most time during 1995 was the merger with the Leeds. On 25 January 1995 Halifax was hit by severe weather in the afternoon resulting in six inches of snow. The ensuing traffic gridlock in and around the town centre meant that there was little point in trying to leave for home. Around nine o'clock in the evening and feeling hungry Geoff Jackson, Dick Spelman, James Crosby and myself trudged through the snow to a local curry house. During the course of the meal the conversation turned naturally to the prospective merger and Crosby, half in jest, remarked that one of the reasons he had come to the Halifax was because they were too big to be involved in a merger. Outsiders may have thought it was a takeover of the Leeds, but internally it was certainly being sold as a merger.

A get together was organised for the two sets of executives, everyone viewing with special interest the body language and nuances of Blackburn as he greeted his ex-colleagues from the Leeds. Certainly a kiss for Judy Aitchison (General Manager marketing for the Leeds) was more than could be expected by any of the 100 per cent male Halifax executive! A few days later Spelman came into my office saying that he had just seen Blackburn, Boyes and Miller walking down the corridor together and for one moment he thought that what was happening was a takeover of the Halifax by the Leeds - and in certain respects this is what did happen.

The message being sent out was that there was great synergy between the administrative excellence of the Halifax and the marketing flare of the Leeds. Whilst it had already been decided to call the merged Society the 'Halifax' it was seen as extremely important to keep the Leeds 'Liquid Gold' brand and their 'Home Arranger' a facility that supposedly took all the hassle out of moving house.

Blackburn put Miller in charge of the programme to integrate the two organisations, which was a surprise considering that the Leeds was much less diverse in its operations than the Halifax and also because Miller himself had only two years' experience of the building society world. In sharp contrast to the Halifax approach, Miller was a great believer in buying in IT solutions, seeing them simply as a commodity. He had previously spoken on public platforms castigating the Halifax IBM Assembler strategy and was also critical of the Halifax approach as being too focused on delivering high quality administration systems. Challenges obviously lay ahead regarding the integration of two totally different development cultures, but the role Miller had been given scotched any ideas that the Halifax was in fact taking over the Leeds. Heading up the Halifax's input into the integration exercise was Mike Ellis, who had been heavily involved in the successful merger discussions, but on his own admission was not a man who was at all conversant with the technicalities of the organisation's administration.

Blackburn was thus using the merger to challenge the need to have experienced administrators in charge at a senior level. However, there were experienced people on the ground in both organisations who worked together to provide a remarkably successful merger of the administrative systems on the first day of the new organisation, 1 August 1995.

The new board structure was expanded to accommodate Sir Timothy Kitson as joint Vice-Chairman along with Prue Leith, Derek Cook and Arnold Ziff who were all previous Leeds non-executive directors. Roger Boyes became the Group Finance Director, taking over from Gren Folwell who moved over to become Managing Director, Building Society. John Lee had been appointed Personnel Director in 1994 and it was announced that Derek Taylor (Managing Director HEAL) would retire in May 1996.

The Chairmen's Committee for the Halifax/Leeds merger.
Sitting left to right: Mike Blackburn, Malcolm Barr, Jon Foulds. (Standing, left to right): Howard Briggs (Secretary to the Committee), John Wood, Gren Folwell, Sir Timothy Kitson, Roger Boyes, John Miller.

Thus with John Miller becoming Business Strategy and Operations Director the powerful executive board members consisted of three ex-Leeds (Blackburn, Boyes and Miller), one outsider (Lee) and one ex-Halifax (Folwell). Foulds had certainly made his mark and accomplished his objective of bringing in new blood.

From day one of the merged organisation it was possible to go into either an ex-Leeds or ex-Halifax branch, and conduct business for a savings account from either organisation. New savings, banking, mortgage and personal loan accounts conducted at any branch were all channelled through to the Halifax mainframe systems. This had been achieved by rolling out the Halifax XCEL system into all the ex-Leeds branches and developing a link between the two Societies' mainframes. Interestingly the link was only achieved by the inherent flexibility of the Halifax's systems being written in IBM Assembler language. In spite of this reliance from day one on the Halifax's systems the debate went on for some months and indeed years as to whether the combined organisation's systems should be based on those from the ex-Halifax, ex-Leeds or a brand new platform.

A truly remarkable presentation to the executive committee took place in the old Leeds Head Office by an IBM sales team in the June of 1995. IBM were proposing that all the Society's IT savings and banking systems could be based on a package called Provida which they were now marketing as their mainline banking product. Miller was particularly keen on the IBM Provida package, having already invested several million pounds in its customer information data base component.

The software had been developed for the Nordic market and essentially provided little more than a simple database and transaction accounting system. It had not been sold to any UK bank, provided no support for UK cheque and credit clearing, nor BACS clearing, nor the LINK shared ATM network. It did not interface with any of the Society's 10,000 terminals nor any of its many other accounting or management information systems and had not been scaled up to support a customer base of even a tenth that of the Society. Apart from that it was fine but of absolutely no interest to the Halifax and was being used by IBM to sell their consultancy services.

Given that the Halifax had over the past decade invested in several hundred man years of effort of its best people in developing a full money transmission service, it was somewhat surprising that Provida was even considered. Two years later Miller was featured in a three-page article in Computer Weekly where he was quoted as 'spending £400 million and throwing out the old Halifax legacy systems' which would be replaced by new mortgage systems from Unisys and savings bank systems from IBM. The article had a familiar ring to it with such phrases, as 'the old Assembler code will eventually be consigned to history'. It continued by stating, 'The Halifax system relied on a home-grown transaction processing monitor which was single threaded'. It is difficult to know which monitor is being referred to, but it certainly could not have been TD01 (Teleprocessing Daily programme number 01), Halifax's remarkable online transaction system, first developed in 1971 by Fred Dawson (Wakefield branch and Head Office computer department), and which was capable of processing over 10 million transactions a day.

As the Halifax reached its 150th anniversary in 2003 there was no sign of any of the new 'promised land' systems from IBM or Unisys. Assembler code was still being used to develop and maintain the old Halifax transaction processing systems (including TD01) that incredibly were supporting over 25 million customers including those migrated from both the Leeds and Bank of Scotland. Systems that had been attacked, criticised and written off many times over the previous two decades were still providing sterling service!

Blackburn and Miller were also keen to make more use of the services of management consultants. Previous Chief Executives had used them, but in a limited way and often to set the scene or justify a change in structure at the start of their tenure. Whitehouse in particular had been very wary of salesmen from the large IT firms trying to sell their general consultancy services. He realised how easy it was for chief executives and directors to be sucked into believing their undeliverable but extremely expensive and disruptive promises. Working on a consultancy contract for the Halifax had additional benefits in that the consultants could go to other banks and building societies informing them about the initiatives of the home loans market leader. Visiting salesman, who were presenting to Whitehouse, would barely get through their pitch associated with their first presentation foil before he would interject with:

> Please don't bother telling us how you see the financial services industry going and how your consultancy arm can help us. We know much better than you how to run our business.

The off balance salesman could then be observed bypassing his first 10 foils as he tried to regain his composure. Whilst the responsibility for employing such consultants obviously lay with the organisation itself the morals of many of these consultancy firms were often questionable. This was especially true of the large accountancy firms whose consultancy arms operated under totally different ethical standards to those of their audit divisions.

1 August 1995 was obviously just the start of the work involved in the merger. In November 1995 the executive committee went off for two days to the Devonshire Arms at Bolton Abbey to review their role. Tensions and differences arising out of the recent merger were still evident with one ex-Leeds heavyweight nearly coming to blows with one ex-Halifax heavyweight. Crosby received a rebuke from the external facilitator, Margaret Exley, for showing a lack of interest in the proceedings and openly reading his newspaper. Nevertheless, decisions were made including one to look at actively reducing headcount numbers within the various merged divisions and branch network. This decision entailed much work for John Lee and his team who put in place attractive redundancy packages (up to two and a half years' salary payoff, plus pension enhancement for early retirement) and also counselling facilities for 'displaced personnel'.

The initial brunt of the upheaval was felt by the branch network, which was already contracting prior to the merger. Indeed the role of the branches was changing fast with the introduction of telephone and business administration centres and the automation of many of the loan underwriting decisions.

Head Office jobs were now spread between Leeds and Halifax, and although enforced commuting was not always popular, the proximity of the various offices meant that no one had to move house just in order to retain their job. Prior to the merger, in general, all central administration jobs were located at various offices within Calderdale. As the number of jobs diminished in one area, often because of the increasing use of IT, other jobs were created in new and expanding areas such as cheque processing and personal loans. Calderdale was thus able to supply sufficient personnel of the right calibre to satisfy the organisation's needs. In future, however, especially with further mergers and acquisitions to come, the organisation's central administration and Head Office jobs would be distributed throughout the country.

Once the merger had been completed rapid conversion to plc status was all-important. Members, whose principal reason for voting for the merger was to receive their due share allocation, were now impatient to 'get their hands on the money'.

The scale of the operation was indeed vast and many adjectives and analogies were used to try and express its size. One of the best was heard in the boardroom from Professor John Kay who said that as far as he knew it was simply the 'biggest give away the world has ever known'. A basic distribution of 200 shares was allocated to every qualifying investor, borrower, employee and pensioner. In addition to this there was a variable distribution comprising two shares per £100 investment balance up to a cut off point of £50,000.

Two thirds of borrowing members and three quarters of investing members voted and not surprisingly 97 per cent of these voted in favour of conversion. How many people read or understood the detailed arguments for conversion, whether a plc is more accountable than a mutual organisation and whether the Halifax would have converted if it were not for the Leeds merger are all issues open to debate. There is, however, no question that the ideals and objectives of those members who helped set up the organisation in 1853 were a world apart from the vast majority of those who voted on the conversion. By the time vesting day, 2 June 1997, arrived 8.26 million members were on average better off to the tune of £2,300 this being the result of a gigantic giveaway of £19 billion.

11

1997 - 2003

With the conversion to plc in 1997 came the end of the Halifax Building Society, the former society now being called the 'Halifax'. The advice given by Rothschilds back in 1988 still held true in that things would never be the same again once conversion had taken place. Shareholders' interests were now the most important and what they wanted to see were plans to grow the business, increase in share value being regarded as just as important as dividends. In spite of HFSL long-term savings business providing 7.5 per cent of the profits and consumer credit and non-mortgage related general insurance a further 2.5 per cent each, the remaining 87.5 per cent of the profit was generated by traditional building society operations. Mortgages were still the mainstay of the business with the Halifax having 19 per cent of the UK residential mortgage market.

The marketplace competition that led to savings products being sold purely on price in the 1980s was to do the same to mortgages in the 1990s. The decline in property values during the first half of the 1990s had the effect of limiting growth in net mortgage lending (gross mortgage lending less repayments and redemptions).

Competition for mortgage sales created a market in remortgages, where borrowers were offered better terms than could be obtained from their existing lenders. The value of remortgages expressed as a percentage of total gross lending went up from 16 per cent in 1993 to 45 per cent in 2003.

Fixed rate mortgages, which started to gain popularity in the late 1980s, also encouraged borrowers to review their mortgage providers at the end of fixed rate terms. As remortgage business grew, all lenders were having to work harder just to retain their existing share of the market. Against this background it was surprising to observe Halifax's dismissive attitude towards this market. In the 1997 Report and Accounts, mention was made of not 'trading at heavily discounted prices in the remortgage

Calum Macaskill presents a Rolex watch to Ronnie Parkinson in 1985 for 15 years of service as Golf Circle secretary.

Dramatic opening to the 1987 X Factor national conference in Harrogate with the unveiling of the new Halifax logo which emerged from a cloud of dry ice.

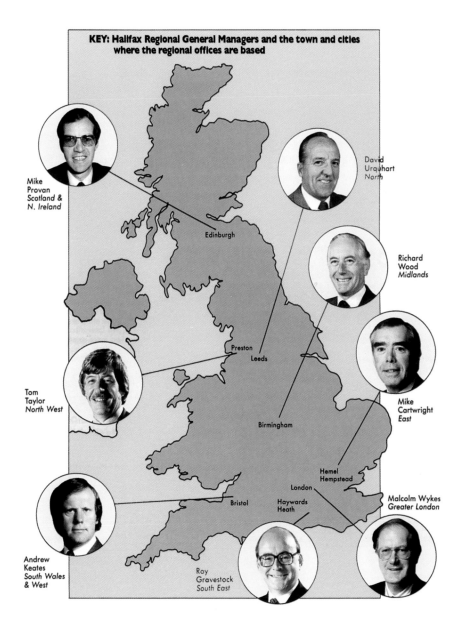

KEY: Halifax Regional General Managers and the town and cities where the regional offices are based

Mike Provan
Scotland & N. Ireland

David Urquhart
North

Richard Wood
Midlands

Tom Taylor
North West

Mike Cartwright
East

Andrew Keates
South Wales & West

Malcolm Wykes
Greater London

Roy Gravestock
South East

Edinburgh

Preston

Leeds

Birmingham

Hemel Hempstead

London

Bristol

Haywards Heath

Regional structure – 1988

The corporate identity of Halifax Property Services in the early 1990s used a distinct green colour along with the Halifax 'X'

One of the spectacular 'people' adverts of 1991

Mike Riley and his head office debt recovery team in 1993

Mike Blackburn and Liz Dawn (*Vera Duckworth from Coronation Street*) both receive honorary degrees from Leeds Metropolitan University in 1998

IF drives home new ID

Jim Spowart and James Crosby at the launch of IF

HBOS 2003 Group Management Board

Left to right: Phil Hodkinson, Andy Hornby, Colin Matthew, James Crosby, Mike Ellis, George Mitchell, Ian Kerr

market', whilst at the same time reporting that the Halifax's net interest margin had increased from 2.27 per cent to 2.48 per cent. The massive loss in share of net mortgage lending, as depicted in the charts below, would have been unacceptable when the Halifax was a mutual building society. However, widening the margin on the existing mortgage book was one way for the plc to improve profitability in the short term.

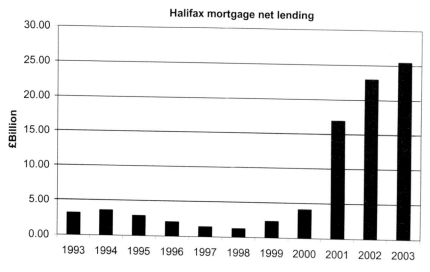

Halifax mortgage net lending

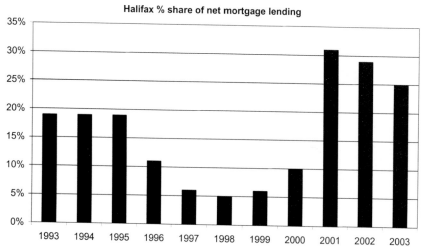

Halifax % share of net mortgage lending

Further acquisitions were an alternative way of growing the business and in 1998 a 50 per cent shareholding in Lex Vehicle Leasing was announced along with the approval of the members of Birmingham Midshires Building Society to be acquired by the Halifax (to be completed in the Spring of 1999). Birmingham Midshires at 7 per cent the size of the Halifax was unlikely to cause too much excitement and it was decided to operate it as a separate entity using its name as one of a portfolio of brands designed to meet differing needs of the market.

Plans were also announced in 1998 to return £1.5 billion to shareholders, this being surplus to the company's requirements. In October 1998 Mike Blackburn announced his intention to step down as Chief Executive, but to remain on the board for a further year, acting as Vice Chairman. Without a doubt his major achievements were the merger with the Leeds and the conversion to plc. James Crosby took over as Chief Executive from 1 January 1999 with John Miller (responsible for mortgages and IT) leaving the Halifax board on 31 December 1998. Changes continued thick and fast through 1999 with Lord (Dennis) Stevenson taking over as Chairman in July. Jon Foulds had been Chairman for eight years during which time dramatic changes had been experienced. Throughout his time with the Halifax he had two obsessions, namely:

◆ to change the 'man and boy' (ie, a lifetime's employment) culture of the organisation

◆ to move away from being just a mortgage bank.

Without doubt he achieved his first objective and made progress with

Dennis Stevenson Chairman 1999

his second. Stevenson had been introduced to Foulds by Blackburn and was also well known to Crosby through their joint involvement in J Rothschild Assurance and St James's Place Capital. His main business interest was Pearson plc where he was Chairman and he also held several non-executive directorships including The Economist Newspapers Ltd. He was one of the two outside members of the Takeover Panel appointed by the Governor of the Bank of England to represent industry.

The all-important chemistry between Chairman and Chief Executive seemed to be there from the start with Stevenson stating:

> The main reason I accepted the job was a strong belief in the management team, in particular James Crosby.

Stevenson's other comments in the 1999 Report and Accounts were open and enlightening. Whilst paying tribute to the contributions of the retiring Foulds, Blackburn and Folwell (Deputy Chief Executive) he cast serious doubt on the value of the recent merger strategy by stating:

> ...the belief that consolidation is guilty until proven innocent; not that we would be so purist as to resist an opportunity to create shareholder value via a consolidating acquisition or merger, but the hard evidence is that they tend to remove value rather than to create it, and that the opportunity cost of diverting management from running the business is very high.

He continued with an inference about certain elements of the organisation's management:

> ....the application of world class management to an industry that is not known for it in the belief that however mature a sector, superior management will always improve results; hence the appointment of Andy Hornby at the age of 32 to lead all Halifax's retail activities.....

Youthful in looks and attitude, Hornby was regarded as a 'whizz kid'. Crosby recruited him from his previous position of managing director of George, ASDA's clothing business. Prior to that he had worked for Boston Consulting Group and Blue Circle. Another claim to fame was that he obtained an MBA from Harvard where he graduated top of his class.

The third strand of Halifax's new strategy that Stevenson highlighted was to join the 'dot.com' revolution with the creation of *IF* (Intelligent Finance) - bringing in Jim Spowart from Standard Life to set up the operation.

IF was to offer direct and online services only, with similar products to the Halifax brand ie, current accounts, savings, mortgages, personal loans and credit cards. It was, however, to operate as a separate company with its own capital backing and provisions for losses in the first few years as the business was built up. This approach would allow it to be very competitive on pricing without causing too much criticism from existing Halifax customers. Setting up their own administration systems and thus duplicating many of the core Halifax systems (which were starting to

Andy Hornby as Chief Executive,
Halifax Retail in 2000

provide interfaces to the Internet) was more difficult to understand. However, at the time **IF** did not want to be constrained by Halifax's old legacy systems and the lack of resources for any new developments due to the Year 2000 workload. Complementing **IF** and Spowart was the recruitment of Peter Wood to set up 'esure', a new and separate Internet general insurance business.

Crosby had started off his term of office with a real bang but he still had to tackle the problem of the below market share of net mortgage lending. He did not need a top Harvard graduate to tell him that the current strategy was going nowhere fast, but Hornby's undoubted expertise and experience would be an integral part of the solution.

In the new environment of price sensitive mortgage products, the largest player in the market must be able to compete, even if that meant reducing margins. The dramatic turnaround of the net mortgage lending position from 1999 onwards (see previous net lending charts) is explained to a large extent by the reduction in the group net interest rate margin. The chart below depicts the reducing margin of the total business, something that Crosby pointed out would be the consequence of going for growth.

Unfortunately, the whole of the mortgage market had become increasingly complicated with many of the best deals being given to new customers, relying on the inertia of existing customers to provide a disproportionate part of the profit of the overall mortgage book. In 2001 Halifax introduced (in line with certain other lenders) an additional, lower variable mortgage rate (HVR2 – interest calculated daily) which it used as

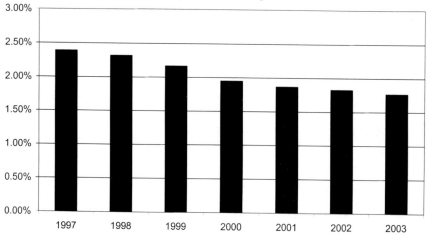

Group net interest margin

its basis for all new variable rate mortgages. The old higher rate (HVR1 – interest calculated yearly) was used for existing borrowers who could, if they contacted their branch and signed new terms and conditions, change to the lower HVR2 rate. Although these existing borrowers were informed of the situation by advertisements and a 'rolling' programme of letters, the morality of the dual rate system was questionable and received some bad press.

In January 2002 the Halifax lost an appeal against a ruling by the Financial Ombudsman that it was wrong to keep some types of mortgage holders on higher rates while offering cut-price loans to new customers. The Halifax, like many other lenders, was caught in a cleft stick in that it wanted to offer better deals to existing customers who were about to move their business elsewhere, but was not unhappy to retain other existing customers on higher rates. The truth of the matter was that the market had changed to such an extent that many borrowers showed no loyalty to their lender and were often referred to in the press as 'rate tarts', a somewhat unkind term for those who switched their mortgages regularly. It was therefore not surprising that the lenders in turn showed diminished loyalty towards their customers. At least the Halifax had aggressively entered the remortgage market and had started to counter criticism from existing borrowers by asking them to come into the branch in order to review their mortgage conditions in the light of new and possibly better priced products.

This recapturing of its share of the intensely competitive mortgage market was not without its cost as the profit generated by retail banking grew modestly from £1,340 million in 1997 to £1,698 million in 2003. These profits excluded exceptional items but included provisions for bad debt. The relevant part of the retail operations of Birmingham Midshires and Bank of Scotland operations were also incorporated in 1999 and 2001 respectively and hence it can be seen that the nature of the retail bank whose profits are being analysed had changed significantly over the period 1997 – 2003. Nevertheless from 2001 the retail bank was growing, increasing its market share and providing many of the customer relationships for the successful insurance and investment arm of the business.

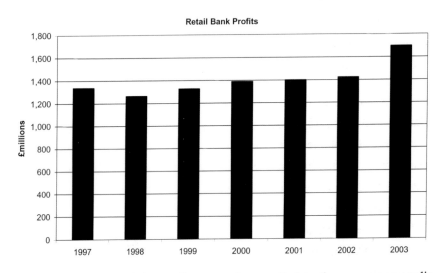

Retail Bank Profits

An aggressive pricing policy was also applied to the consumer credit products (credit cards and personal lending), again with the objective of growing the business, this also being helped by acquisitions such as Bank One Corporation in June 2000. As successful as this policy was, these products still only accounted for less than 5 per cent of the Retail Bank's profits by the turn of the century. Driven by the desire to control costs, Hornby priced the savings and banking products to give the best deals to customers who were willing to use more efficient ways of doing business with the Halifax (eg over the phone and via the Internet). Numbers of branches and agencies were reduced, as was the number of teller positions in many of the remaining outlets. More ATMs were installed and high transaction activity accounts were encouraged to use the re-launched (October 2000) current account that paid a very competitive 4 per cent interest on credit balances.

This push towards greater use of ATMs and banking products was in many ways a return to the strategy of the late 1980s and early 1990s. Current accounts were seen as a key product with great potential for cross selling and the major clearing banks were targeted with aggressive marketing campaigns. In the first few years of the new millennium HBOS was opening over one million new bank accounts every year, representing around 25 per cent of the 'new and switchers' market.

In the announcement of the launch of *IF* it was stated that the business would start operating in the summer of 2000 and that the scale of the investment would be £100 million. As the 'dot.com' euphoria reached its peak at the start of the new millennium, the people in the independently set up company were confident of exponential growth, with the talk of even outgrowing the parent company in the fullness of time.

Not surprisingly for a company that was reinventing everything the Halifax had taken 150 years to develop, the launch was delayed - until October for telephone access and December for the Internet channel. More people were drafted in from the core bank to help with the business and by the end of 2001 *IF* was part of the Retail Bank reporting into Hornby. Losses before tax of £88 million, £154 million, £147 million and £53 million were reported for the years 2000 to 2003, but break even was reached in the last month of 2003. *IF* was successful at bringing in the business, for example contributing a massive £5 billion of net mortgages in 2001. It was similar to many other start up banks in that it could offer very attractive interest rates initially in order to buy the business and build up an asset base. The trick of course is eventually to make a profit on those assets without losing too many of them. Spowart moved on from *IF* in 2002 and left HBOS in 2003, having set

Howard Brown makes it to the front cover of the 2000 Report and Accounts

up one of the largest Internet banks and also pioneering the concept of offset banking. The reduction in *IF*'s operating costs are no doubt the key to its long-term success.

Throughout his tenure at the Retail Bank, Hornby accelerated its change in culture from being administrative and service led, to one where sales and asset growth were the number one objective. Not only did he ensure that the products were price competitive, but he also instigated the successful advertising campaigns featuring Howard Brown who was a member of staff at the Halifax Sheldon branch in the Midlands. So successful was Howard as the face of the Halifax, especially in TV commercials, that it was he rather than Hornby, Crosby or Stevenson who was in demand to launch campaigns, open buildings and present trophies. Understandably, for a man who had been brought in to such a senior position at such a young age, Hornby also brought in many other younger people from outside the organisation. It should be noted, however, that Hornby's appointment is not unique. In 1903 Enoch Hill was appointed as Secretary to the Halifax, at the then relatively tender age of 37. Hill remained in charge of the Society for 35 years, was knighted for his services to the industry and saw the Halifax's assets increase by a factor of 60.

Peter Burt
Group Chief Executive Bank of Scotland
prior to formation of HBOS in 2001
(Courtesy of HBOS plc)

Crosby's desire to obtain more of the group's profits from the diversified business was helped no end in 2001 by the merger with the Bank of Scotland and the formation of HBOS. Peter Burt, Bank of Scotland's group Chief Executive, realised that his bank would not achieve its full potential on its own and during 2000 he had lost out to Royal Bank of Scotland in a bid to take over NatWest and then later on in the same year had failed to put together a merger with the Abbey. Third time lucky, the ensuing discussions with Halifax resulted in an announcement on 4 May 2001 with the merger becoming effective on 10 September 2001.

Announced as a merger of equals, there was indeed sense and synergy in the deal that allowed Stevenson and Crosby to argue that this particular consolidation did create shareholder value. Historically there had been good links between the two organisations with the joint credit card venture in the late 1980s and the secondment of commercial banking experts in 1990 to help sort out the problems the Halifax encountered after entering the commercial lending market. Bank of Scotland's strengths in business and corporate banking complemented Halifax's strength in retail banking. Geographically the branch networks complemented each other, much more so than with the Halifax/Leeds merger. Culturally it was stated that there was also great similarity, but in truth the Halifax had experienced much greater recent change and an influx of younger outside senior management.

In order to make any merger a success there has to be give and take from both sides and this was shown by the new corporate Head Office being sited at the Mound, Edinburgh. However, as regards the allocation of jobs Halifax came out on top by providing Stevenson and Crosby as Chairman and Chief Executive and Mike Ellis, with his experience of mergers, as Finance Director. Roger Boyes (ex-Finance Director) and John Lee (ex-Personnel and Communications Director) retired on the formation of HBOS. Burt took up a position as Executive Deputy Chairman for a year but his main contribution was in bringing the two organisations together.

Blackburn's legacy was maybe not so much the Halifax/Leeds merger but more the fact that he made the Halifax management aware of their own abilities in implementing such mergers. This time round they had the benefit of recent experience and decisions that took years with the previous merger were now taken in months. In bringing together the various divisions of the two organisations mention was made that the merger 'brings together two of the most conservative Treasury operations in the city'. This comment was no doubt made for comparison with the Abbey and their disastrous treasury operations when they went into the 'junk bond' end of the market. Crosby acknowledged how crucial IT integration would be over the next three years with Burt stating that there was not much philosophical difference between the two organisations' IT strategies, even though BOS had recently gone down the outsourcing route which was in complete contrast to the Halifax's philosophy. The BOS outsourcing operation was reversed under HBOS, and a detailed plan was put together to replace BOS retail bank systems with those from the Halifax. This conversion obviously took time, which is hardly surprising when one realises that the Leeds mortgages were only just being transferred onto Halifax systems in 2001.

Whilst Colin Matthew, George Mitchell and Gordon McQueen from BOS were the executive directors responsible for Business Banking, Corporate Banking and Treasury, Andy Hornby was made the executive director for Retail Banking. Phil Hodkinson, recently recruited from Zurich Financial Services, was the executive director in charge of Insurance and Investment. The old Halifax organisation fitted into several arms of the new group structure - obviously it made up a large component of the Retail Bank but it also provided major contributions to Treasury as well as Insurance and Investment. This latter division had continued to grow, not just by organic growth and diversification but also by acquisition - eg controlling interest in St James's Place Capital in 2000 and Equitable Life's 2001 operating assets.

At the end of 2003 it started to underwrite its own household insurance, thus moving away from earning commission from Royal Sun Alliance - a move which would eventually generate bigger profits but which ended a long-term relationship. From £271 million of profit in 1997 it moved to £887 million in 2003, this providing 23 per cent of those of the group – thus illustrating the success of Crosby's diversification strategy.

Since taking up the Chief Executive position, Crosby had a clear vision of the way forward for the organisation – one that he kept to over the years. He saw great potential for growth in all areas of the business. Often this could be done organically at the expense of competitors and assisted by suitable acquisitions - or maybe by a merger should a suitable opportunity arise. This growth relied on satisfying three objectives:

- ◆ provide customers with good value, absolute transparency and quality service
- ◆ motivate and provide good incentive schemes for the workforce
- ◆ create value for the shareholders.

Trying to satisfy all parties was a tall order that could create conflicts of interests. It did, however, demonstrate that he had ambitious but realistic aims for an organisation the size of HBOS. By implication these objectives meant that HBOS must be the lowest cost provider in all of their business areas. This could be brought about by economies of scale and the sensible use of technology – two things for which the late Halifax Building Society had been noted. It was as if the last decade had been a story of two mergers. The first was an end in its own right, the second was a means to an end – that of meeting Crosby's growth aspirations.

12

50 YEARS OF CHANGE

The changes that occurred in the Halifax over the 50 years since its centenary were brought about by factors both external and internal to the organisation. In 1953 it was a cautious, administratively-led organisation seeking to provide affordable home ownership for as many people as possible. By 2003 it had changed into a diversified provider of financial products and was led by the desire to increase sales and profits.

During all this time the roles of the organisation's Chairman and Chief Executive were paramount and it was their decisions that set it apart from its competitors. Sometimes this leadership exhibited a 'steady as we go' direction and at other times they decided when and how to embrace changes such as the introduction of information technology, product diversification and new or different retail outlets for the organisations products.

In 1953 the Society's branch network was one of its major assets and although occasional mention has been made of the network, it is beyond the scope of this book to do justice to its history and the individuals involved. The 115 branches that the Society had in 1953 were all local clones of the main branch in Halifax, but of varying sizes.

The Society's Chief Officials (Executive in modern day parlance) of 1953 included the branch managers from Bradford Bank Street (W Kenworthy), Huddersfield (C B Jackson), Leeds (N Longbottom), Liverpool (D Lawrence), Sheffield (M H Denham) along with the London District manager (G Jennings). They were important men and were brought up to Head Office to discuss policy matters and provide feedback on local variations in the mortgage and savings market. Every branch was responsible for its own customer accounting and establishing good contacts with the local solicitors, estate agents and accountants.

Whilst certain high profile and city branches received visits from Head Office personnel, many other branches saw nobody from one year to the next except of course for the visit from the branch inspection team. Most branches had a chief clerk, only a handful having an assistant manager, and it was this level of management that ran the day-to-day operation of the branch. If the branch manager had a competent chief clerk he was free to spend a fair proportion of his time 'marketing' the Society at Rotary luncheons, in gentlemen's clubs or on the golf course. He may, however, have preferred to spend most of his time in the office; the choice was his, as to a large extent he was his own master.

The Society had its fair share of characters in these branch management positions, all with their own idiosyncrasies. Harry Smart of Edinburgh, for instance, was an early advocate of cutting costs wherever possible. He discovered that a standard Halifax passbook was only just over the weight limit for a normal letter and therefore instructed his staff to cut off a tenth of an inch from the bottom of every passbook that required mailing back to a customer. A letter was sent to Head Office suggesting that all branches could adopt this initiative. The succinct reply back from Head Office stating, 'Mutilation of passbooks will cease forthwith', left him in no doubt as to their thoughts on his idea.

Ken Coates, whilst serving as the Halifax branch manager in the 1970s, had to attend a Head Office marketing course designed to encourage managers to get out of the office and make more contact with potential business introducers. Ken was noted as being a social animal and on being told that they should all aim to spend at least two days a week out of the office indicated that he didn't intend to cut down for anyone.

There was, in general, good bonhomie between the branch managers, many of whom had seen service together in their careers at various branches. If an employee was ambitious about a career in the branch network and wanted to end up managing one of the Society's premier branches, he may well have had to move five or six times and uproot the family to live in different parts of the country. In Albert Thayre's days he personally masterminded all the moves and if an employee refused any more than one offer of promotion it could well signify the end of his career progression.

Nor was Head Office excluded from these moves, it being seen as not only a good supply of potential managers but also as a staging post for managers in their career development. People like Peter Wood, born and bred in Halifax and initially recruited at Head Office, saw service in Edinburgh, Southport, Liverpool, Hyde and Manchester before returning to Halifax to manage the flagship branch. He eventually ended up being promoted to Chief Inspector and then moving over to be an Assistant General Manager in the marketing division. By contrast the amiable and humorous Ronnie Parkinson had a career based at Head Office where he ended up as an expert in mortgage matters. Although he provided advice and guidance to the most senior of the Society's employees he never achieved the same status as some of his peers who had moved through the branch network. Others started their careers out in the branch network and ended up in senior positions at Head Office, the most successful of these being Calum Macaskill and latterly Geoff Jackson and Dick Spelman. However, as the twentieth century progressed this promotion route became increasingly harder to follow, as Head Office became the domain of large departments of specialists.

The introduction of the Society's first computer systems in the 1960s heralded the start of a long, slow demise in the importance of the branch. Whilst the automation of the posting of transactions to customers' accounts was seen as a godsend by many branches, others realised that they had lost the responsibility for an essential piece of administration. There was also a reversal in roles in that head office could now statistically analyse the centrally held computer files and report back to branches on the level of investors and mortgage business.

In 1953 the vast majority of customers had to make regular branch visits to pay money in or take money out, either in the form of cash or cheques. Fifty years later the vast majority of customers preferred to use ATMs, the facilities of a current account and credit and debit cards to perform the same transactions. The advent of the Internet and much more use of the telephone reduced the need to visit branches even further, resulting in branches principally becoming an outlet for the selling of new products. Even in the selling of the all important mortgage products, the branches role in underwriting had been diminished with the introduction of credit scoring systems. Whilst the responsibility of the branches had changed, the pressures on the staff working in this environment had no doubt increased as they strove to meet their selling targets, finding themselves not only competing against external players but also internal, centralised direct selling operations.

The top ten societies in 1985 just prior to the changes brought about by the new 1986 Building Societies Act were:

Halifax
Abbey National
Nationwide
Woolwich Equitable
Alliance & Leicester
Leeds Permanent
Anglia
National Provincial
Bradford & Bingley
Britannia

The changes that had been experienced by the Halifax were obviously not unique and it is interesting to view these in relation to what had happened to other building societies. In 1953 there were 782 societies, this reducing to 65 in 2003. This reduction in the number of societies was brought about to a large extent by the increasing costs of compliance and IT systems both of which favoured the larger organisations with their economies of scale. Many of the remaining smaller societies argued that they were satisfying a local need with their regional presence. This may be true but their traditional branch offices and lack of electronic money transmission services came at a cost making them unattractive in the interest rates they charged. Given the increasing importance of being price competitive in the world of the twenty first century it is difficult to see anything other than a further reduction in their numbers. Even the large and middle ground societies nearly all experienced mergers and rationalisation.

By the turn of the century only the Nationwide (who merged with the Anglia) and the Britannia remained as building societies. Bradford & Bingley converted to a plc, National Provincial was taken over by the

Abbey National, Leeds Permanent merged with the Halifax and the Woolwich was taken over by Barclays. Alliance & Leicester also converted to a plc and acquired Girobank. Of the five remaining banks/building societies the outstanding mortgage balances in 2003 were:

HBOS	£171 billion	(£20 billion in 1985)
Abbey	£88 billion	(£16 billion in 1985)
Nationwide	£71 billion	(£8 billion in 1985)
Bradford & Bingley	£26 billion	(£3.1 billion in 1985)
Britannia	£14 billion	(£2.7 billion in 1985)

What had, however, changed was that the major clearing banks had aggressively entered the residential mortgage market such that their outstanding mortgage balances in 2003 were:

Lloyds	£71 billion
Barclays	£62 billion
Royal Bank of Scotland	£48 billion
HSBC	£25 billion.

With the conversion to plc of the Abbey, along with the clearing banks involvement with mortgages, the role of the BSA as industry spokesman was becoming less relevant. In 1989 Jim Birrell and David Gilchrist of the Halifax were influential in the formation of the CML (Council of Mortgage Lenders), which operated out of the same building as the BSA but once again truly represented all the major players. HBOS was, however, still the dominant lender in 2003 and the big three building societies of 1985 (Halifax, Abbey National and Nationwide) were still major lenders but had adopted quite different strategies over the intervening 18 years.

The Abbey was the first building society to convert to plc status in 1989, under the leadership of Peter Birch the Chief Executive. Prior to conversion some new blood had been brought in, such as Gareth Jones from Redland to head up their treasury department. Seeking to grow the business they adopted a strategy of moving towards generating a third of their profits from traditional ex-building society business, a third from new business, such as life assurance, and a third from treasury operations.

All went well until in 2001 Abbey made the first of several bad debt provisions for junk bond dealing. As the extent of the bad debts became apparent heads rolled - Jones in 2001 and Ian Harley the Chief Executive in 2002. These bad debts had a dire effect on the competitiveness of their mortgage products as they sought to widen margins to help offset losses in their treasury operations. The above mortgage balance figures for 2003 show that the Nationwide had nearly caught them up and the comparative ratio with the Halifax had dropped from 80 per cent to 50 per cent. Other factors, such as changes in top management and unsuccessful merger negotiations, all contributed to this loss in share of their traditional retail business. The Abbey, which had been such a respected competitor for so many years, was in a sorry state by the time the Halifax was celebrating its 150th anniversary.

The Nationwide by contrast committed itself to remaining a mutual building society. Brian Davis its Chief Executive argued that they were big enough to have the required economies of scale and because they did not have to pay shareholders a dividend they could be particularly competitive on interest rates and also provide exceptional service. They fought several high profile cases, including one to encourage the industry not to charge for ATM withdrawals. Whilst they have undoubtedly provided stiff competition for the mortgage banks, it is debatable how relevant their case for mutuality is in the world of the twenty first century. There are those who argue that it is only a matter of time before one of the members' attempts to force the Nationwide to convert to plc status is successful.

The Halifax's conversion to plc status was forced upon it by the requirements of the merger with the Leeds Permanent. If conversion had not occurred then, it would quite likely have occurred before its 150th anniversary. The pressures for constant growth which come with being a plc bring with them a much riskier operating environment, as can be seen by the events that took place at the Abbey. So far the Halifax and its successor HBOS has done well in this new environment, where plc status has helped with its diversification and mergers and acquisitions strategies. It would have been impossible in 1953 to envisage how much the organisation would grow and change over its next 50 years. One can only wish them well and look forward to the next 50.

Appendix 1

Presidents/Chairmen

Algernon Denham JP	President	1945 - 1961
Ian AD Maclean	President (*Chairman from 1973*)	1961 - 1974
Sir Raymond Potter	Chairman	1974 - 1983
Richard Hornby	Chairman	1983 - 1990
H Jon Foulds	Chairman	1990 - 1999
Lord Dennis Stevenson	Chairman	1999

Chief Executive

Fred Bentley	General Manager	1949 - 1956
Sir Raymond Potter	Joint General Manager	1956 - 1960
Edwin Beresford	Joint General Manager	1956 - 1960
Sir Raymond Potter	Chief General Manager	1960 - 1974
Albert J Thayre CBE	Chief General Manager	1974 - 1982
John O Spalding CBE	Chief General Manager	1982 - 1985
John O Spalding CBE	Chief Executive	1985 - 1988
Sir James Birrell	Chief Executive	1988 - 1993
J Mike Blackburn	Chief Executive	1993 - 1999
James Crosby	Chief Executive	1999

Appendix 2

Assests of Halifax and Building Society Movement

Assets
£million

1,000,000
100,000
10,000
1,000
100
10
1

1953
1954
1955
1956
1957
1958
1959
1960
1961
1962
1963
1964
1965
1966
1967
1968
1969
1970
1971
1972
1973
1974
1975
1976
1977
1978
1979
1980
1981
1982
1983
1984
1985
1986
1987
1988
1989
1990
1991
1992
1993
1994
1995
1996

Year

■ Halifax □ Movement

Appendix 3

Annual increase in assets of Halifax

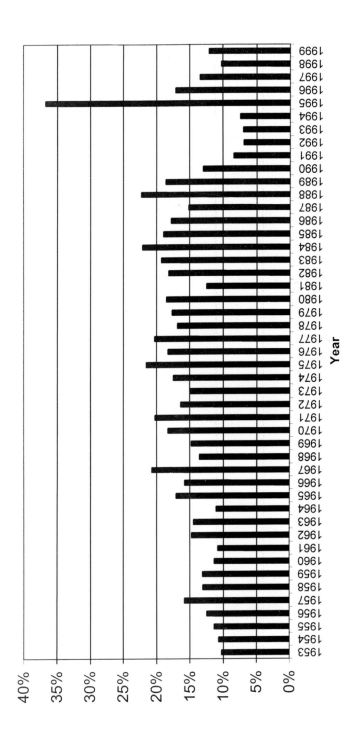

Year

Appendix 4

Halifax Assets as % of the Building Society Movement

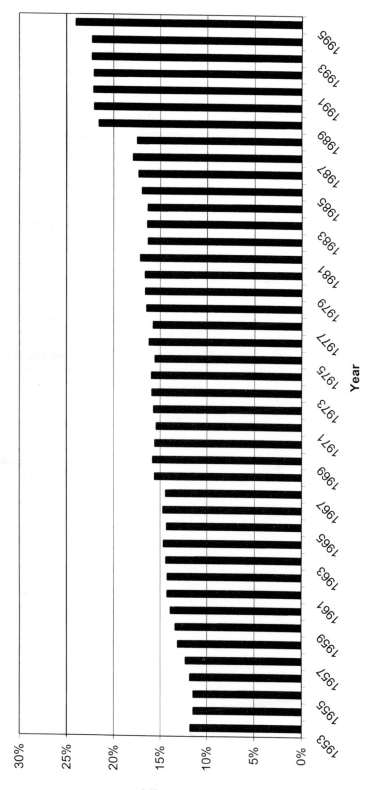

Year

Appendix 5

Asset Size of Abbey National as a percentage of Halifax

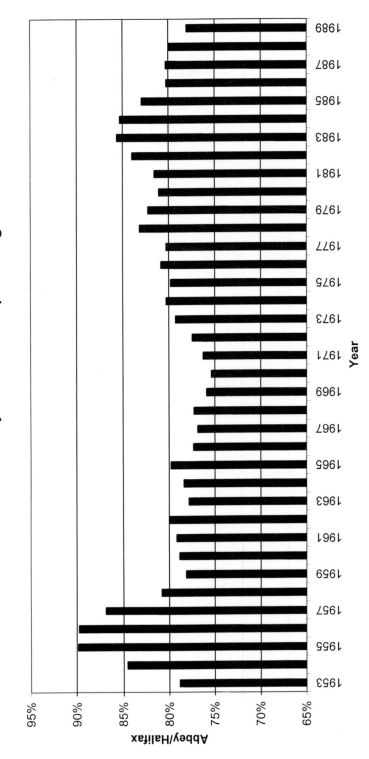

Appendix 6
Retail Price Index

Appendix 7
Bank Rate (Maximum within year)

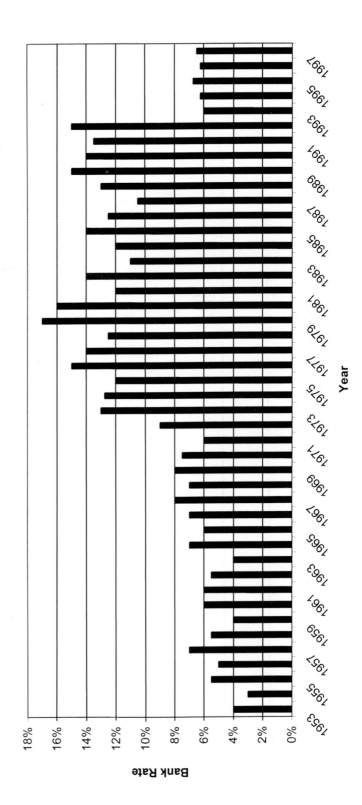

Appendix 8

BSA Recommended Investors' Share Rate

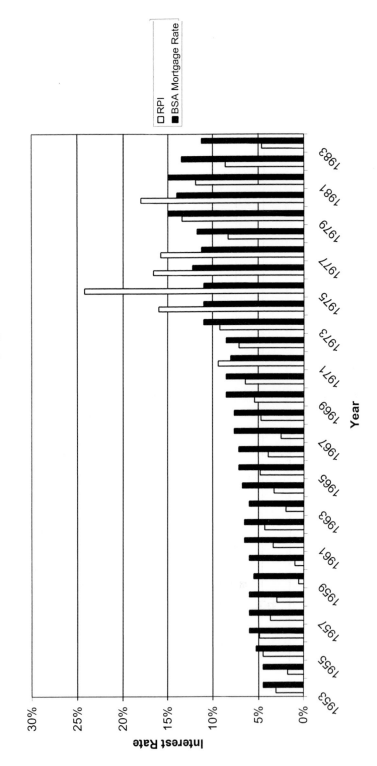

Appendix 9

BSA Recommended Mortgage Rates

Appendix 10
House Price Inflation

Appendix 11

Halifax Branches

(includes ex Leeds but not Bank of Scotland)

INDEX